breathe

THE LIFE-GIVING OXYGEN OF THE LORD'S PRAYER

KAREN HODGE

DISCIPLESHIP MINISTRIES

Published by:
Committee on Discipleship Ministries
1700 North Brown Road, Suite 102
Lawrenceville, Georgia 30043
Bookstore: 1-800-283-1357
www.pcacdm.org/bookstore

Although many publishers do not capitalize terms, and particularly pronouns which refer to the Trinity, in this study CDM publications has capitalized those elements for clarity of reference.

ISBN: 978-1-944964-68-9
Cover Designer: Mary Davis
Layout Designer: Helen Jimmie Weigt

Contents

Introduction

Breathe

"To be a Christian without prayer is no more possible than to be alive without breathing."
Martin Luther[1]

Take a deep breath and exhale. Refreshing, right? Breathing is very complex but is primarily a subconscious activity. Did you know an average person breathes in and out around 22,000 times a day? Oxygen is the body's life-giving gas. It is crucial to help boost our immune system and overall health. Our sensitive brains require lots of oxygen to think. When your oxygen levels dip and you get lightheaded, concentrating can be hard. We often don't think about breathing until we can't catch our breath.

There is a danger in familiarity. We may become casual in our relationship with God, taking His presence for granted. Martin Luther said, "To be a Christian without prayer is no more possible than to be alive without breathing." Prayer is a lifeline for believers. It is the life-giving means God designed to build our relationship with Him and others. He created it to be an ongoing conversation, starting with His speaking to us through His Word and our responding to Him in prayer. It would be ridiculous to think you would only need to breathe one hour, one day a week. Paul admonished us to "pray without ceasing" (1 Thess. 5:17). Prayer ought to be the natural overflow of our time in Scripture. As spiritual infants, the more our Father speaks to us, the more we will begin to mimic His words. As we grow and mature in truth, the healthier and more robust will be our walk with Christ. These means of grace are as inextricably entwined as breathing in and breathing out. Cutting off these vital lifelines means we are more susceptible to the schemes of the father of lies. But the good news is when we are in trouble, God is only a prayer away. We need only to cry out, "Help, Lord!" Spiritual vitality begins with inhaling truth and exhaling prayers.

The deeper we breathe, the stronger we grow. For years I studied voice, and the core exercise of vocal training is breathing techniques. Learning to breathe deeply from your diaphragm enables you to sustain notes and sing on key. The deeper the singer breathes, the more she exercises this muscle and then becomes a stronger singer. Spending time in God's Word and prayer is our daily, life-giving breathing exercise. The more we enjoy Him and build our relationship through prayer, the stronger our spiritual muscles will be for serving in His kingdom.

The Bible is the truth-saturated voice of God to our very soul. Every single word in the sixty-six books is God-breathed (2 Tim. 3:16). God is truth (Isa. 65:16). Jesus is the truth (John 14:6). And the Holy Spirit is the Spirit of truth (1 John 5:6). If for a minute we doubted whether we could trust His words fully when fears and trials impede, Jesus reminds us, "Sanctify them in the truth; Your word is truth" (John 17:17). We are not smart or clever enough to understand His Word or converse with Him in prayer on our own. We must have the Spirit's help.

The first inspired description of the Spirit is found in Genesis 1:2. "The earth was without form and void, and darkness was over the face of the deep. And the Spirit of God was hovering over the face of the waters." The word for Spirit here is "breath or wind." God created man through a breath. "The LORD God formed the man of dust from the ground and breathed into his nostrils the breath of life, and the man became a living creature" (Gen. 2:7).

Before Christ redeems us, we do not just struggle to breathe; we are dead in our sins. Nicodemus asked Jesus a question that was a matter of life or death: "How can a man be born when he is old?" Jesus answered, "Truly, truly, I say to you, unless one is born of water and the Spirit, he cannot enter the kingdom of God. That which is born of the flesh is flesh, and that which is born of the Spirit is spirit. Do not marvel that I said to you, 'You must be born again.' The wind blows where it wishes, and you hear its sound, but you do not know where it comes from or where it goes. So it is with everyone who is born of the Spirit" (John 3:4-8). We need the same life-giving breath from heaven to live as faithful followers.

Enrolling in the School of Prayer Together

At the beginning of Jesus's early ministry on a mountainside outside of Capernaum, He shared the teaching we call the Sermon on the Mount. We study it in Matthew 5–7. Jesus was teaching His followers the kingdom of God is not about a list of rules we are to follow legalistically but rather is an invitation to a relationship He has framed with grace for us to be conformed into His image. It is not about externals and self-righteousness, but it zeros in on what is going on in the heart. Right in the middle of the sermon, He offers an oasis of grace. It is a daily pattern on how to commune with the Father. Jesus is not focused on how we pray but what we pray. These words lay the groundwork for our vertical relationship with the Father and our horizontal relationships with those around us. The first three petitions cast our eyes upward towards God's name, reign, and kingdom. The last three petitions extend horizontally towards how God will meet our material, spiritual, and relational needs. God's glory above our needs—this is the ideal order of prayer.

I am excited for us to learn to pray together.

How To Use This Study

Jesus gathered a group so they could learn how to pray together. Why would we think we could learn any other way? As we will see, there are no singular pronouns in the entire prayer. It is covenantal, or relational, through and through. I want to encourage you to study, pray, and live this out together. Our grand purpose is to consider in the context of community what it might look like if the words of the Lord's Prayer were written over every aspect of our lives, homes, work, church, and community. It is a short passage, but we will be amazed at the rich learning-layers found as we gaze at the multifaceted truths together. It is good for us to slow down, read, pray—and take a deep breath.

Each Weekly Chapter Offers

TEACHING

Weekly Focus and Identity Themes

We will offer complimentary video-teaching, but even better, consider asking a team of women in your local church or neighborhood to lead you through the study.

BREATHING EXERCISES

Bible Study Homework and Prayer Journal

We will spend time each day inhaling God-breathed truths. We will consider how our position in Christ determines our posture in prayer.

We encourage you to spend time exhaling what He teaches you in prayer by making space to reflect on it in your prayer journal. This Bible study and prayer journal are designed to be very interactive. Pick up your Bible and your favorite colored-pens and enjoy filling the pages of this book.

PRAYER PROMPT

Each day your prayer prompt will apply an age-old prayer model to the content we are learning:
ACTS - Adoration, Confession, Thanksgiving, and Supplication.

Each week will also include a confessional question and answer about prayer as well as time in the Prayer Book of the Bible, The Psalms.

WEEK	FOCUS	IDENTITY Learning to pray as . . .	PASSAGE
1	Position & Posture	Dependent Daughter	Matthew 6:5-8
2	Proximity	Interdependent Sister	Matthew 6:9a
3	Presence	Holy Pilgrim	Matthew 6:9b
4	Priority	Loyal Steward	Matthew 6:10
5	Provision	Grateful Neighbor	Matthew 6:11
6	Protection	Forgiven Follower	Matthew 6:12-13

P.S. We are excited to offer a downloadable children's curriculum, *Building on the Lord's Prayer*[2], so you and your family can learn to pray together across the generations.

Let's study and pray together!

1 Martin Luther as quoted in George Sweeting, *Talking it Over* (Nashville: Thomas Nelson, 1985), 88.

2 https://www.pcabookstore.com//p-6276017-building-on-the-lords-prayer-a-six-week-study-pdf.aspx.

Week One:
Position & Posture

Learning to pray as a Dependent Daughter

Matthew 6:5-8

Teaching

WEEKLY FOCUS & IDENTITY THEMES

Matthew 6:5-8

And when you pray, you must not be like the hypocrites. For they love to stand and pray in the synagogues and at the street corners, that they may be seen by others. Truly, I say to you, they have received their reward. But when you pray, go into your room and shut the door and pray to your Father who is in secret. And your Father who sees in secret will reward you. And when you pray, do not heap up empty phrases as the Gentiles do, for they think that they will be heard for their many words. Do not be like them, for your Father knows what you need before you ask Him.

Our Position in Christ Determines Our Posture in Prayer

Throughout the years, we have been blessed to have many of our friends adopt children into their families. Each addition has added a layer of thanksgiving as they became living pictures of how our Father God chooses us, not because of our merit but out of sheer grace. The Thomas family taught me another dimension that struck me to the heart. We hosted them for dinner when they returned home with their beautiful daughter from Kazakhstan. We asked them questions about their experience. We asked them to describe the orphanage. They began by describing the old building and then went on to talk about the staff and children they had met. They told us of the overwhelming smell of the cabbage cooking. But then they shared something I will never forget. They said, "It was eerily quiet except for the very creaky red door." I was shocked: "In a building full of babies?" They explained the babies had ceased crying because they had been conditioned that no one would come and feed or change them when they cried. My heart broke at this unhappy picture—the deafening silence of an abandoned orphan. As I looked across the table at our new covenant child, I was simultaneously overjoyed and convicted.

Pretending Hypocrites

Jesus starts the school of prayer by reminding the disciples it is not *if* but *when* they pray. Prayerlessness is as foolish as trying to exist without breathing. Prayer can often be forgotten or only used as a last resort. Why? Because we prefer self-sufficiency, actively seeking control of a situation. Putting together a well-developed plan seems more efficient. Waiting on the Lord can be inconvenient. Jesus is our Father, and He knows what His children need to learn. They need to learn to pray. Prayer is to be our *first* resort—a vital lifeline for every moment of our day. Prayer begins as an orientation or posture of our hearts and lives.

Our position in Christ will determine our posture in prayer. Prayer is forward-facing dependence. It is actively seeking God's face. Prayer challenges us as followers of Christ to embody the Latin phrase *coram deo*, which translated means "as a believer we live life in the presence of, under the authority of, and for the glory of God."[1] Prayer is encompassed in adoration, confession, thanksgiving, intercession, and supplication.

Our posture is not just physical but also spiritual. It is an orientation of our hearts that determines our prayers. Jesus begins the school of prayer with a stunning contrast so we will not be confused. Throughout Scripture, we see people kneel or lie prostrate. In verse 5, we see a hypocrite's posture is to stand in the fear of man for the purposes of self-glory. The word *hypocrite* originally was a theatrical term meaning to wear a mask or play a part. Their stage is a synagogue where they can be esteemed for their devotion and religious activity. They also posture themselves publicly on street corners so that they may be seen by others. Hypocrites are practical atheists in their prayer life. Hypocrites act like orphans living as though their Father does not exist. Their prayers are filled with empty words and are focused outward rather than upward. We see a fundamental disconnect in their hearts between what they profess and what they possess. But the Father unmasks and exposes these pretenders. Their aim is to be seen not by God but by man. God allows them their heart's desires. The passing praise of men is their singular reward.

How about you? Do you wear the mask of religious popularity? Do you try to polish your prayer with just the right words to convince others you are more of a devoted follower than you actually are? How do you know if you are praying like a hypocrite or a dependent daughter? The answer lies in who gets the glory.

> Prayers that are meant for the ears of others will never reach the ears of God.
>
> Spiros Zodhiates[2]

> What is deadly to the church is when the external forms of religion are maintained while their substance is discarded. This we call practical atheism. Practical atheism appears when we live as if there were no God. The externals continue, but man becomes the central thrust of devotion as the attention of religious concern shifts away from man's devotion to God to man's devotion to man, bypassing God. The "ethic" of Christ continues in a superficial way, having been ripped from its supernatural, transcendent, and divine foundation.
>
> R.C. Sproul[3]

Dependent Daughters

Jesus will address us corporately as He moves into teaching us His prayer, but in verse 6, He is addressing us as individual children. The inner room of a home is the place where valuables or treasures are stored. All children of God have an inner room or prayer closet. The question is whether we go in or stay outside. Imagine the immediate connection a little child experiences when she steps into her Father's room. He is waiting there expectantly. His posture as the door opens is to extend His open arms in love. Imagine this inner room as an intimate, private place. It is modest with no windows. Its simplicity brings focus and clarity, leaving the distractions of the day at the door. It is a place where you leave your reputation behind and, instead, rest. What do you bring into the room? You bring your praise and your petitions. The ever-present invitation is to come quickly and often. It is a place where you are seen, known, and dearly loved. You can sit at the feet of the Master Intercessor where He intercedes for you, and you can intercede for others. The inner room is a treasure room. It's the place where treasures from Christ are waiting for you. The riches of His grace, compassion, wisdom, and love are accessible. It is a holy habitation where a little child and the loving Father commune.

Babbling Babies

I have had the privilege to travel with Susan Hunt and a team of women's ministry leaders to minister in Japan. We traveled to seven cities in ten days. At the center of each of these communities, you would find a Buddhist temple. I was fascinated by the architecture and the large trees and bell towers outside these shrines. Devoted Buddhist followers would come to the temple and write their prayers on slips of paper and then tie them to the tree branches. Afterward, they would ring the bell so that Buddha would be alerted to their prayers. The temple tree was covered with these prayer-filled papers in each town, and we often heard bells tolling.

Jesus now contrasts the prayers of dependent daughters with another type of orphan-like prayer. To the Jews of Jesus's day, Gentile prayers sounded like the mindless babbling of a baby. Babies mimic the sounds they hear from adults over and over again. We, too, may utter traditional words or rote prayers like verbose mantras. These prayers are aimlessly thrown into the wind rather than towards God. The danger of babbling prayers is the lack of heart and mind engagement. Genuine prayer should be the overflow of the Christ-centered heart and mind, and this type is the overflow of an insecure and immature person. God is never impressed with our many words. He looks to the sincerity of our hearts. As we continue our study and explore the Lord's Prayer, we must be careful not to recite this prayer in a rote or incantational way. Remember the adage: familiarity breeds contempt.

I Need Thee Every Hour

I need Thee every hour,
Most gracious Lord;
No tender voice like Thine
Can peace afford?

Refrain:
I need Thee, oh, I need Thee;
Every hour I need Thee;
Oh, bless me now, my Savior,
I come to Thee.

I need Thee every hour,
Stay Thou nearby;
Temptations lose their power
When Thou art nigh.

I need Thee every hour,
In joy or pain;
Come quickly and abide,
Or life is vain.

I need Thee every hour,
Teach me Thy will;
And Thy rich promises
In me fulfill.

Robert Lowry and Annie Hawks[4]

Not Rules and Ramblings, but a Relationship

Watching the Thomas family adopt their daughter was a classroom in Covenant Theology for our church. Covenant Theology is a biblical framework to understand the special relationship between God and His people. They prayerfully and joyfully chose their daughter from the other side of the world. The pursuit of bringing her into their family was costly, lengthy, and well-planned. Their daughter was not chosen based on what she could give her parents but solely on unconditional love. Becoming a member of their family required legally changing her name. At that moment, she went from orphan status to beloved daughter. She immediately had access to all the rights and privileges that were afforded to her as a member of the Thomas family. We are beloved daughters of the King and have been adopted into the Family of families. His adoption plan for us was predestined before the foundation of the world (Eph. 1:5).

Our condition was far direr than the orphanage in Kazakhstan. God set His electing love on us when we were orphans of the Fall, enemies of the cross, and children of wrath. We were adopted not because of our merit or works but solely by His grace. Crying out to God as *Abba* (Rom. 8:15), Father, or Daddy is never conditional on what we have or have not done on a given day. We can cry out to Him in prayer because we have been redeemed through the blood of the Lamb. Our status has moved from orphan to daughter, from a slave of sin to freedom in Christ. His adoption of us (as unworthy as we are) is at the heart of the gospel. Our adoption is not about us; it is all about our Father.

Our position in Christ as a dependent daughter will determine our posture in prayer. We are to come as a humble and reliant child, yet as a child who does not hesitate but instead runs needy and messy to her Father. At any given moment, daughters can come not only boldly yearning, crying, and lamenting but also confidently asking, seeking, and knocking. We can ask for big things because God is big and for small things because He cares about every detail of our lives. This prayer position of humility is the antithesis to a self-orientation. Bowing to Him rids our lives of self-reliance, self-rule, and selfish desires. The inner room is where, on our knees, the battle is wrought for who will have authority, control, and influence. Will it be me or Thee?

Prayer=Helplessness

God wants us to come to Him empty-handed, weary, and heavy-laden. Instinctively we want to get rid of our helplessness before we come to God . . . Prayer is bringing your helplessness to God . . . The very thing we are allergic to—our helplessness—is what makes prayer work. It works because we are helpless. We can't do life on our own. Prayer mirrors the gospel. In the gospel, the Father takes us as we are because of Jesus and gives us His gift of salvation. In prayer, the Father receives us as we are because of Jesus and gives us His gift of help.

Paul Miller[5]

Weekly Prayer List

Write the Lord's Prayer over your life this week. Spend time writing out your prayer requests in these four areas. Come back to this list daily to continue to ask, seek, or knock. Put a star next to answered prayers. And then on day seven, reflect and praise God for what He has done and allow the remaining items to shape your prayers for next week.

Our Father in heaven, hallowed be Your name. Your kingdom come, Your will be done, on earth as it is in heaven. Give us this day our daily bread, and forgive us our debts, as we also have forgiven our debtors. And lead us not into temptation, but deliver us from evil (Matt. 6:9-13).

Personal Prayer

Family Prayer

Church Prayer

Prayer for my neighbors (work or community)

Day One: The Problem of Prayerlessness

How would you describe your current prayer life? (circle one)

Non-existent Sporadic Growing Vibrant

INHALE GOD'S WORD

Read	Note the Prayer Postures (action verbs)
Matthew 7:7-8	
Jeremiah 29:12-14	
Colossians 4:2-3	
1 Thessalonians 5:16-18	

Now ask the Lord to make these the daily postures of your life.

EXHALE IN PRAYER ~ ADORATION

Dear Lord, I worship you as my Father . . .

GO BACK TO YOUR WEEKLY PRAYER LIST AND SPEND TIME IN PRAYER.

Day Two: Position & Posture

INHALE GOD'S WORD

Read	List all the Family Words
John 1:12-13	
Romans 8:14-17	
Galatians 4:4-5	
Ephesians 1:4-6	

EXHALE IN PRAYER ~ ADORATION

Dear Father, I praise You for bringing me into Your family and for these covenantal blessings:

GO BACK TO YOUR WEEKLY PRAYER LIST AND SPEND TIME IN PRAYER.

Day Three: Pretending Hypocrites & Babbling Babies

Understand your prayer default. Write your own comparisons.

Orphan-like Prayer	Daughter-like Prayer
Independent	Dependent
Prayer as a last resort	Prayer as your first line of defense
Flashy public prayers with little private prayer	Frequent prayer which overflows into public prayer
Anxiety-driven prayer	Adoration-oriented prayer
Plan first and pray later	Pray first and plan as an overflow

INHALE GOD'S WORD

Read Luke 18:9-14. Write in your own words a description of the posture of the...

Pharisee:	Tax Collector:

Now read Luke 18:15-17 and write the benefits of coming as a dear child.

EXHALE IN PRAYER ~ CONFESSION

Dear Father, I confess my poor postures in these areas of my life. . .

GO BACK TO YOUR WEEKLY PRAYER LIST AND SPEND TIME IN PRAYER.

Day Four: Pretending Hypocrites & Babbling Babies

INHALE GOD'S WORD

Read Titus 1:15-16. Prayerfully examine the gap in your life between what you say you believe about God and how you live. This gap, the hypocrite's posture, is to stand in self-reliance looking for the approval of man.

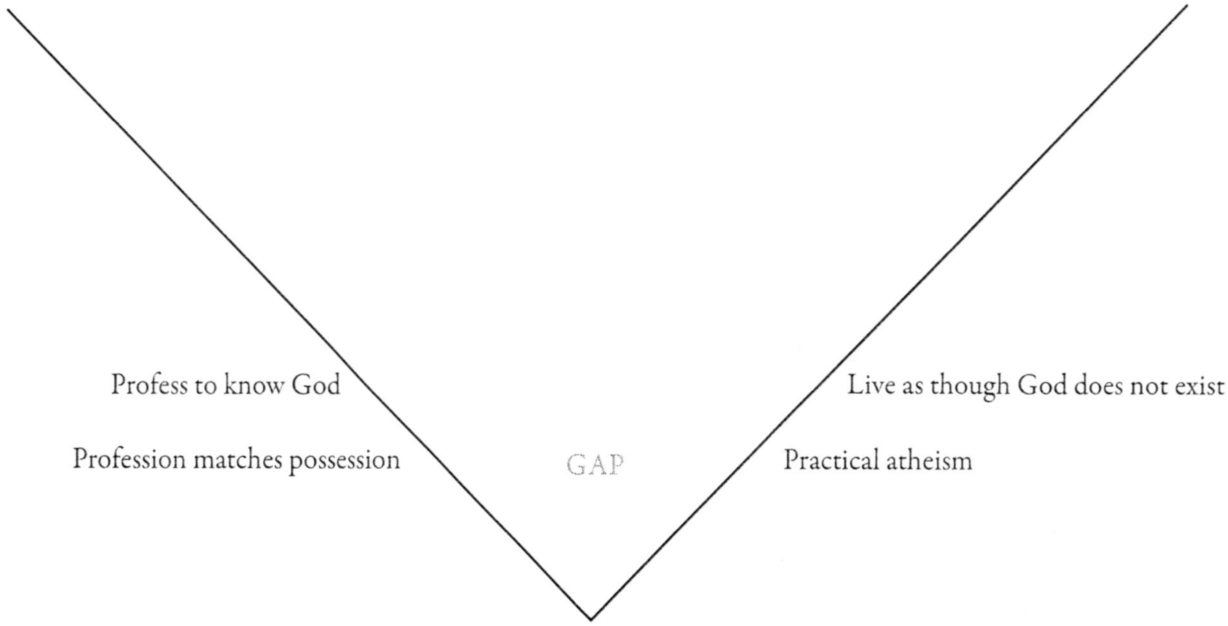

List specific ways in the gap above where you have lived as a . . .
- PRETENDER: Times you have worn a mask or played a part.
- APPROVAL CRAVER: Ways you have lived in the fear of man, seeking others' approval.
- LOOK AT ME!: Words you have spoken or deeds you have done this week to be seen by others.
- GLORY HOUND: Areas of your life you have taken credit for instead of giving glory to God.

EXHALE IN PRAYER ~ CONFESSION

Dear Father, I repent of my desire to be seen by others as . . .

GO BACK TO YOUR WEEKLY PRAYER LIST AND SPEND TIME IN PRAYER.

Day Five: Prayer Book – The Psalms

INHALE GOD'S WORD

Read Psalm 8 and fill the first arrow with the scriptural descriptions of our covenantal, relational LORD and fill the second arrow with the ways Scripture describes mankind. Note any contrasts in the middle.

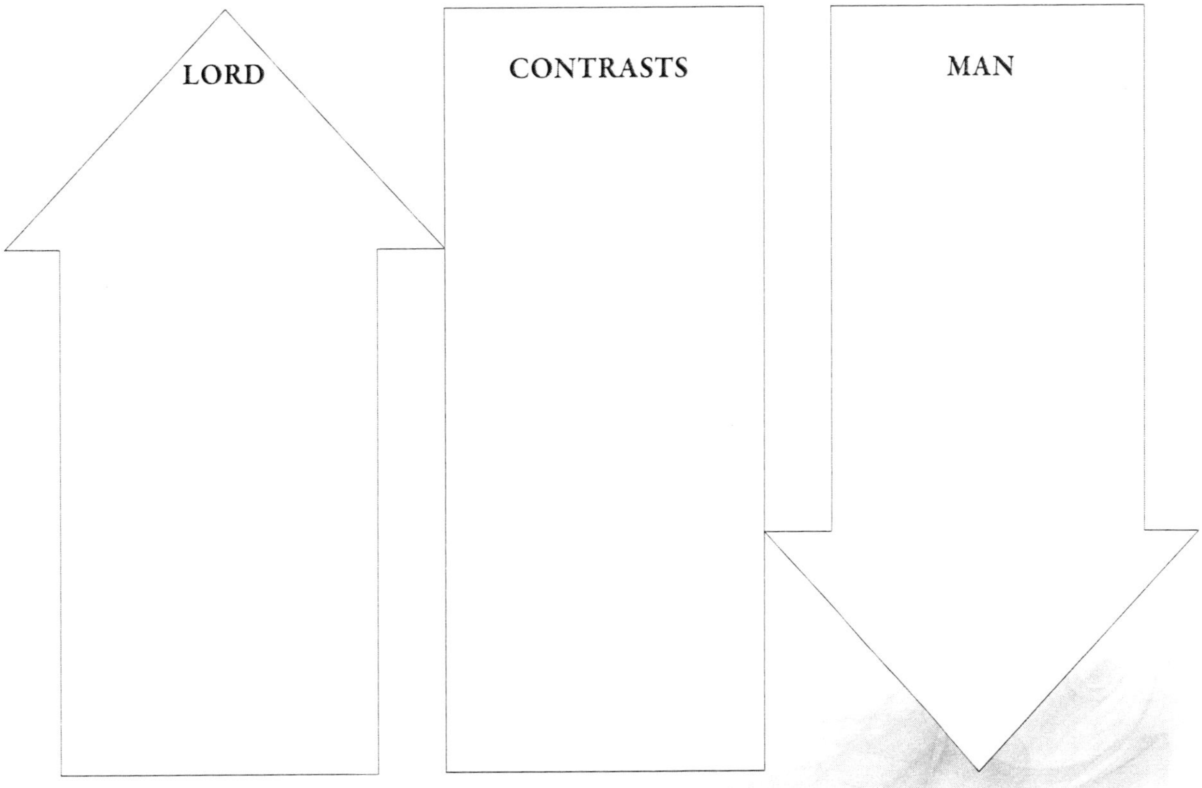

EXHALE IN PRAYER ~ THANKSGIVING

Dear Father, I am thankful for these many blessings this week:

GO BACK TO YOUR WEEKLY PRAYER LIST AND SPEND TIME IN PRAYER

Day Six: Dependent Daughter

INHALE GOD'S WORD

Read through the *Westminster Confession of Faith*, Chapter 12, on adoption and circle the benefits of being a dependent daughter. Spend time reading the scriptural proofs.

God guarantees the adoption of all those who are justified in and for the sake of His only Son, Jesus Christ (Eph. 1:5; Gal. 4:4-5). Those adopted enjoy the liberties and privileges of God's children (Rom. 8:17; John 1:12), have His name put on them (Jer. 14:9; 2 Cor. 6:18; Rev. 3:12), receive the Spirit of adoption (Rom. 8:15), have access to the throne of grace with boldness (Eph. 3:12; Rom. 5:2; Heb. 4:16), and are enabled to cry "Abba, Father!" (Gal. 4:6). They are pitied (Ps. 103:13), protected (Prov. 14:26; Ps. 27:1-3), provided for (Matt. 6:30, 32; 1 Peter 5:7), and disciplined by Him as a father (Heb. 12:6). They are never cast off, however (Lam. 3:31-32; Heb. 13:5), and are sealed until the day of redemption (Eph. 4:30) and inherit the promises (Heb. 6:12) as heirs of everlasting salvation (1 Peter 1:3-4; Heb. 1:14).

EXHALE IN PRAYER ~ THANKSGIVING

Dear Father, I am thankful to You for the following benefits which I am privileged to access as a dependent daughter.

GO BACK TO YOUR WEEKLY PRAYER LIST AND SPEND TIME IN PRAYER.

Day Seven: Writing His Prayer over Your Life

INHALE GOD'S WORD

Read back through our passage for this week, Matthew 6:5-8.

What are three takeaways that you learned this week through your personal study, prayer journaling, or your small group discussion?

1.

2.

3.

EXHALE IN PRAYER ~ SUPPLICATION

Dear Father, would You write Your prayer over my life, family, church, and neighbors.

RETURN TO YOUR WEEKLY PRAYER LIST

- Place a star next to answered prayers.
- Spend time giving praise to God.
- Reflect upon His persevering grace for what remains on your prayer list.
- Ask God to apply what you have learned this week as you seek His face to write your prayer list for next week.

---

1 R. C. Sproul, "What Does Coram Deo Mean?" Ligonier.org (November13, 1997), https://www.ligonier.org/learn/articles/what-does-coram-deo-mean.

2 Spiros Zodhiates, *The Lord's Prayer* (Chattanooga, TN: AMG Publishers, 1998), 5.

3 R.C. Sproul, "What Is Practical Atheism?" Ligonier.org (January 12, 2015), https://www.ligonier.org/posts/practical-atheism-vs-biblical-christianity.

4 Annie Hawks and Robert Lowry, "I Need Thee Every Hour," in *Trinity Hymnal* (Suwanee, GA: Great Commission Publications, 2021), 674.

5 Paul Miller, *A Praying Life* (Colorado Springs, CO: Nav. Press, 2009), 54-55.

6 Chapter 12, *Westminster Confession of Faith* (Lawrenceville, GA: CDM, 2007), 56.

Week Two:
Proximity

Learning to pray as an Independent Sister

Matthew 6:9a

Teaching

WEEKLY FOCUS & IDENTITY THEMES

Matthew 6:9a

Pray then like this: "Our Father . . ."

Parenthood

"Daddy!" I cannot count how many times my kids would yell his name as they ran into the house or to the back of the church office. They entered cheerfully and boldly. He dropped whatever he was doing with few exceptions to greet them with a hug. Our children have unconditional access to their dad, even at work. When they were little, we had a jar on his desk filled with sweet treats. When they were teenagers, there was a mini-fridge stocked with their favorite drinks. For as long as it takes to drink a Dr. Pepper, they could shoot the breeze and catch up on the day. He also had a basketball behind the door. A quick game of horse made for fun togetherness.

When God created Adam, He made a covenant of works with him. The promise was God's presence, and the condition was perfect obedience. But one man would not make a family, so God created woman out of man and established the first family unit. He performed the first wedding ceremony and created the most intimate of bonds. Their complementary companionship was His provision for their loneliness. Man and woman as image-bearers reflected the first Covenant community—the Godhead. Their design fueled their purpose and mission to be fruitful and multiply. He elected His family before the foundation of the world to extend the garden to the ends of the earth. Our first earthly parents rebelled and brought brokenness and division into the world. Shame and blame alienated them from one another and God. They hid from God, but the Father came, called, and clothed His kids.

In love, He made provision for proximity. The Covenant of Grace provides a way for us to live in His presence. He promised to send His Son who would be their Redeemer. His protective love banished them from the garden to begin their family expansion. Eve quickly realized her sons were not the promised Seed as brother turned against brother and brought bloodshed into the first family. When the LORD confronted Cain with this evil, Cain said, "I do not know; am I my brother's keeper?" (Gen. 4:9). God in His mercy confronted Cain toward conviction of sin that potentially would bring him near. God was reminding him: "You belong to Me, and you and your brother belong to one another." Instead of receiving God's compassion, Cain responded with callousness. Rather than drawing near, he independently departed to build his own city.

> You can sum up the whole of the New Testament teaching in a single phrase if you speak of it as the revelation of the Fatherhood of the Holy Creator. If you want to judge how well a person understands Christianity, find out how much he makes of the thought of being God's child, and having God as Father. If this is not the thought that prompts and controls his worship and prayers and his whole outlook on life, it means that he does not understand Christianity too well.
>
> J.I. Packer[1]

Proximity

Throughout Scripture God has worked through families. He also made a covenant with Abram. "And I will establish my covenant between Me and you and your offspring after you throughout their generations for an everlasting covenant, to be God to you and to your offspring after you" (Gen. 17:7). Though childless, Abram was promised a family which would number as great as the stars. The essence of the Covenant of Promise is "I will be your God, and you will be My people, and I will live among you." Christ's death on the cross provides the pathway to live in relationship with God and others. As we learned last week, adoption places us in the Family of families. We belong to one another and are designed to be *interdependent*. We are our sister's keepers.

Our vertical relationship means we are united to God. Our horizontal relationships mean we are united to one another. This is our family portrait as the Church as a Covenant Community. The word "Our" in the Lord's Prayer is a plural pronoun. In fact, there are no singular pronouns in the entire prayer. This prayer is a corporate and covenantal prayer. We cannot pray the Lord's prayer for ourselves alone. Our familial bond allows us to cry out in one voice, "Our Father!" Our Father is immanent and near. Next week as we consider, "Our Father in heaven, hallowed be Your name," we will look at how He is also transcendent.

You cannot pray the Lord's Prayer and even once say "I."
You cannot pray the Lord's Prayer and even once say "My."
You cannot pray the Lord's Prayer and not pray for another.
For when you ask for daily bread, you must include your brother.
For others are included in each and every plea.
From the beginning to the end of it, it never once says "Me."

Spiros Zodhiates[2]

Prodigal Kids

Like our first father and mother, Adam and Eve, we are covenant-breakers instead of covenant-keepers. Our desire for lesser things drives us away from the Father. Luke 15 unpacks the rescue of a loving father towards two prodigal sons. One was extravagantly wasteful and the other was pridefully pious. One son squandered all his wealth and the other squandered the privilege of proximity to the father. One was physically impoverished and starving, the other was spiritually needy and hungry. Both were far away from the father. How great was the father's love? While his son was still a long way off, his father saw him. He overlooked his son's filth and extended compassion toward him. The father did not wait for the son to move towards him but, instead, ran headlong toward him with hugs and kisses. This homecoming quickly escalated into an elaborate family feast. The elder prodigal was so angry he chose not to fellowship with his brother or father. He shared a house with his father, but his actions showed he did not share his father's heart. The younger prodigal son shows us the path to restored family fellowship. Repentance is turning toward the Father. Faith takes the first step. Family unity is only possible through a daily rhythm of prayers for repentance and faith.

Parenting

Solomon likened a family to a quiver of arrows (Ps. 127:4-5). Every parent is aiming at a target. Sometimes the trajectory is more influenced by the world than the Word. Ask any parent of a high school senior, and you will hear all about their archery strategy. They may shed a tear or two as they grow sad about having to hold the bow tight and steady. Launching children into adulthood is hitting the bullseye. Letting go is hard but necessary. Maturity is the winning shot!

Our biological children share a strong family resemblance because of our shared DNA. Our children also resemble us as they mimic our words and actions. The similarities can often be convicting. Our prayer is they will look and sound more like their heavenly Father than us.

Our spiritual Parent, God, has a perfect plan for us to grow up. His trajectory is heaven. Maturity will happen through nothing less than total transformation. It will be uncomfortable and inconvenient. It will take a lifetime investment, and there are sure to be tears. As He sanctifies us through His Word and prayer, we will begin to look and act more like our Father. As you and I seek to grow up into maturity, we look up rather than to others. We become what we behold and we are continually becoming what we will be. Paul tells us this maturity journey happens in glory degrees, one from another, until we look like Jesus (2 Cor. 3:18).

Privileges

Our covenant family is a divinely appointed spiritual classroom where we will spend our lives learning about our covenant privileges and responsibilities. Maturing is never a solo act; it always happens in the context of family. God uses our covenant family to shape and mold us. Serving together strengthens our spiritual muscles to step out in faith. A believer's life is not a "Jesus and me" but a "Jesus and we." We grow as we study and apply the Word of God together. Studying the content of the gospel in the context of community is part of the Spirit's transformative process. Corporate prayer, such as praying the Lord's Prayer together on a Sunday morning, lifts our eyes off of ourselves or one another and up to our Father. Feasting around the Lord's Table nourishes us with the reminder: our only hope is in Jesus Christ. These means of grace in the Church are a foretaste of when we will feast forever together at the marriage supper of the Lamb. Experiencing these gifts together changes our perspective from focusing on the temporal to the eternal things.

The Gospels and Epistles are our textbooks, teaching us about "one-anothering." Our relationships stay grounded when they are Word-based. We are given by our Lord the commandment to love one another (John 13:34). Paul elaborates on this throughout his letters as he calls on believers to be devoted to one another (Rom. 12:10), to serve and to bear each other's burdens (Gal. 5:13; 6:2) and to be kind, compassionate, and forgiving of one another (Col. 3:13). Interdependent sisters are committed to this intentional, covenantal one-anothering as we walk along the line that runs from eternity past to eternity future.

Relationally-driven corporate and intercessory prayer are lifelines as we walk through the uncertainty of the now-and-not-yet. Praying for and with one another enables us to live covenantally. Prayer helps us to keep in step with the Spirit as we walk alongside one another (Gal. 5:25). And we are changed as we confess ours sins to one another and pray for our mutual needs (James 5:16). Focusing on the Word helps us coach each other to think biblically about all of life.

Leadership has been defined as "to go in front of or beside another to get them to an intended destination."[3] I think this is also a great definition for gospel discipleship. The intended destination for all believers is heaven, or Home. The invitation to walk is the same as Paul's, "Follow me as I follow Christ" (1 Cor. 11:1). Gospel friends walk shoulder to shoulder with us reminding us what is true. Spiritual mothers are a few steps in front of us in spiritual maturity. We are thankful when they intentionally enter into a nurturing relationship with us younger women to encourage and equip us to live for God's glory. If we look over our shoulder, there are likely others who are following us as we follow Christ. Sometimes we walk many years alongside another while at other times it may be just a few steps. Since Home is our trajectory, we seek to invest in the only things that will exist forever: His people and His Word. Walking each other Home is a sacred and holy covenant-privilege.

In prayer, I am not alone. I am one with the members of God's family, which is also my family. My weak prayer is caught up into the great stream of prayer that goes up forever from God's family. The strength of my prayer is that it is not simply mine; that moment I fall on my knees I am no longer an individual man or woman to align to God but a member of God's family the communion of the saints. That gives life and force to prayer and comfort and confidence to those who pray. On my knees I cannot be alone! My prayer, as weak, as feeble and as helpless as it is, will be united with the prayer of the whole church. We are members of one body. We belong to an association of intercessory prayer.

Spiros Zodhiates[4]

Prepared Place

Chris's office was a special place prepared to welcome our children. Being part of Team Hodge granted them unfettered access. They could enjoy the benefits of fellowship and food because they belonged to him. Jesus's disciples also enjoyed the benefits of fellowship and food with the Father (John 14:1-5). When He told them He was going to leave them soon, their hearts were troubled. They still had growing up to do, so the thought of separation seemed unbearable. Like a parent who is going out for the evening and stoops low to reassure a crying child in the doorway, Jesus promised He was going to prepare a place for them. And even though He would be apart from them for a while, He will return for them and bring them Home. And in the challenging days before He comes, He will not leave them alone. He is leaving them a Helper, the Holy Spirit who will comfort and counsel them until He returns. This Home is being prepared for you and me as well. It is beyond any place we have ever known. It will be a great family reunion. You and I will fellowship with family we have never known from every tongue, tribe, and nation. It is a place where you and I will always be welcome and belong. Jesus has prepared it through His life, death, and resurrection. When we arrive Home, we will cry in one unified voice around the Throne, "Our Father, Abba, Daddy, we love and worship You!" We will be proximate to the Father because we will see Him face to face.

Weekly Prayer List

Write the Lord's Prayer over your life this week. Spend time writing out your prayer requests in these four areas. Come back to this list daily to continue to ask, seek, or knock. Put a star next to answered prayers. And then on day seven, reflect and praise God for what He has done and allow the remaining items to shape your prayers for next week.

Our Father in heaven, hallowed be Your name. Your kingdom come, Your will be done, on earth as it is in heaven. Give us this day our daily bread, and forgive us our debts, as we also have forgiven our debtors. And lead us not into temptation, but deliver us from evil (Matt. 6:9-13).

Personal Prayer

Family Prayer

Church Prayer

Prayer for my neighbors (work or community)

Day One: Parenthood

Both the *Heidelberg Catechism* and the *Westminster Confession* outline the Lord's Prayer. Today spend some time asking yourself these questions and take the time to read the Scripture proofs.

INHALE GOD'S WORD

Reflect upon these questions from the *Heidelberg Catechism* and read the corresponding Scripture proofs.[5]

Q. 117: What is the kind of prayer that pleases God and that He listens to?

A: First, we must pray from the heart to no other than the one true God, revealed to us in His Word, asking for everything God has commanded us to ask for (Ps. 145:18-20; John 4:22-24; Rom. 8:26-27; James 1:5; 1 John 5:14-15).

Second, we must fully recognize our need and misery, so that we humble ourselves in God's majestic presence (2 Chron. 7:14; Ps. 2:11; 34:18; 62:8; Isa. 66:2; Rev. 4).

Third, we must rest on this unshakable foundation: even though we do not deserve it, God will surely listen to our prayer because of Christ our Lord. That is what God promised us in His Word (Dan. 9:17-19; Matt. 7:8; John 14:13-14; 16:23; Rom. 10:13; James 1:6).

Q. 120: Why did Christ command us to call God "our Father"?

A: To awaken in us at the very beginning of our prayer what should be basic to our prayer—a childlike reverence and trust that through Christ God has become our Father, and that just as our parents do not refuse us the things of this life, even less will God our Father refuse to give us what we ask in faith (Matt. 7:9-11; Luke 11:11-13).

EXHALE IN PRAYER ~ ADORATION

Dear Father, I worship because You placed me in the Family of families . . .

GO BACK TO YOUR WEEKLY PRAYER LIST AND SPEND TIME IN PRAYER.

Day Two: Prayer Book—The Psalms

INHALE GOD'S WORD

Read Psalm 84. Fill this house with all the descriptive words of how lovely God's dwelling place is and the blessings of being near the Father.

EXHALE IN PRAYER ~ ADORATION

Dear Father, I praise You for these three or four specific ways You have brought me comfort through the nearness of Your presence this week . . .

GO BACK TO YOUR WEEKLY PRAYER LIST AND SPEND TIME IN PRAYER.

Day Three: Prodigal Kids

INHALE GOD'S WORD

Spend unhurried time meditating on the story of the prodigal sons in Luke 15:11-32.

- Which son do you identify with, and why do you feel this way?

- What are some words or phrases that describe the father's pursuit of the lost son?

- How can you rest in the rescue of the Father's love this week?

EXHALE IN PRAYER ~ CONFESSION

Dear Father, I confess my penchant to run after lesser things such as . . .

GO BACK TO YOUR WEEKLY PRAYER LIST AND SPEND TIME IN PRAYER.

Day Four: Parenting

INHALE GOD'S WORD

Read Romans 12 and reflect on how the Spirit is transforming you through His Word and prayer both in your vertical relationship with God and your horizontal relationships with others in the Body. Under each heading write 4 or 5 ways that you have been changed or transformed over the past year in these two areas.

Vertical relationship with God	**Horizontal relationships with others in the context of community**

EXHALE IN PRAYER ~ CONFESSION

Dear Father, I confess there are these specific areas in my life where I need to grow and mature:

GO BACK TO YOUR WEEKLY PRAYER LIST AND SPEND TIME IN PRAYER.

Day Five: Privileges

INHALE GOD'S WORD

Interdependent sisters are committed to Covenant "one-anothering." Read through all or some of the following passages.

Circle the commands you need to pray about cultivating in your life this week.

Love one another	John 13:34
Honor one another above yourselves	Romans 12:10
Live in harmony with one another	Romans 12:16
Build up one another	Romans 14:19; 1 Thessalonians 5:11
Be likeminded towards one another	Romans 15:5
Accept one another	Romans 15:7
Admonish one another	Romans 15:14; Colossians 3:16
Greet one another	Romans 16:16
Care for one another	1 Corinthians 12:25
Serve one another	Galatians 5:13
Bear one another's burdens	Galatians 6:2
Forgive one another	Ephesians 4:32; Colossians 3:13
Be patient with one another	Ephesians 4:2; Colossians 3:13
Speak the truth in love	Ephesians 4:15, 25
Be kind and compassionate to one another	Ephesians 4:32
Speak to one another with psalms, hymns, and spiritual songs	Ephesians 5:19
Submit to one another	Ephesians 5:21, 1 Peter 5:5
Look to the interests of one another	Philippians 2:4
Bear with one another	Colossians 3:13
Teach one another	Colossians 3:16
Comfort one another	2 Corinthians 1:3-5
Encourage one another	1 Thessalonians 5:11
Exhort one another	Hebrews 3:13
Stir up [provoke, stimulate] one another to love and good works	Hebrews 10:24
Show hospitality to one another	1 Peter 4:9
Employ the gifts God has given us for the benefit of one another	1 Peter 4:10
Clothe yourselves with humility towards one another	1 Peter 5:5
Pray for and confess your faults to one another	James 5:16

EXHALE IN PRAYER ~ THANKSGIVING

Dear Father, I am thankful for these specific sisters You have placed in my life:

1.

2.

3.

4.

5.

GO BACK TO YOUR WEEKLY PRAYER LIST AND SPEND TIME IN PRAYER.

Day Six: Prepared Place

INHALE GOD'S WORD

Read 1 Thessalonians 2:7-8.

What are one or two truths you can share this week?

What are one or two ways you will invest sharing the gospel or sharing your life (time, talents, treasures) with a sister this week?

Walking each other Home is a sacred and holy Covenant privilege.
Write one or two names in each box. Spend time praying for your gospel friends, spiritual mothers, and those who are following you as you follow Christ.

Gospel Friends **Women who walk alongside me:**	**Spiritual Mothers** **Women who have spiritually nurtured me:**

Those who follow me as I follow Christ:	**Gospel Friends** **Women I walk alongside:**	**Spiritual Daughters** **Women I spiritually nurture:**

Discipleship/Gospel Transformation: We are all just walking each other Home.

EXHALE IN PRAYER ~ THANKSGIVING

Dear Father, I am grateful for these spiritual mothers, gospel friends, and for those who follow me as I follow Christ:

GO BACK TO YOUR WEEKLY PRAYER LIST AND SPEND TIME IN PRAYER.

Day Seven: Write His Prayer over Your Life

INHALE GOD'S WORD

Read back through our passage for this week: Matthew 6:9a.

What are three takeaways that you learned this week through your personal study, prayer journaling, or your small group discussion?

1.

2.

3.

EXHALE IN PRAYER ~ SUPPLICATION

Dear Father, would You show me the areas of my life that are out of alignment with Your Prayer . . .

RETURN TO YOUR WEEKLY PRAYER LIST

- Place a star next to answered prayers.
- Spend time giving praise to God.
- Reflect upon His persevering grace for what remains on your prayer list.
- Ask God to apply what you have learned this week as you seek His face to write your prayer list for next week.

1 J.I. Packer, *Knowing God* (Downers Grove, IL: InterVarsity, 1973), 181-182.

2 Spiros Zodhiates, *The Lord's Prayer* (Chattanooga, TN: AMG Publishers, 1998), 46.

3 Def. 1.1. Oxford Dictionaries.com. as used in Karen Hodge and Susan Hunt, *Life-giving Leadership* (Lawrenceville, GA: Committee on Discipleship Ministries, 2018), 150.

4 Zodhiates, *The Lord's Prayer*, viii.

5 G.I. Williamson, *The Heidelberg Catechism: A Study Guide* (Phillipsburg, NJ: P&R Publishing, 1993), 208, 212.

Week Three:
Presence

Learning to pray as a Holy Pilgrim

Matthew 6:9b

Teaching

WEEKLY FOCUS & IDENTITY THEMES

Matthew 6:9b

Pray then like this: "...in heaven, hallowed be Your Name . . ."

Heaven Is Our Home

Over the years, Chris and I have lived in many different cities and homes. The call to the pastorate is the call to be a pilgrim. God called us to move from our South Florida home at the height of the Great Recession. It took six years and nine months to sell our home. During the thirteen years we served at Naperville Presbyterian Church in Naperville, Illinois, we lived in five rental homes. At each new address, God provided an excellent place for us to live and extend hospitality to our congregation. We called them house number one, two, three, four, and five.

I felt like a pastor's home should be not too shiny, too shabby, but somewhere right in the middle. My opinion was house number three was a little too nice to be a pastor's home. One chilly evening I was greeting our guests and hanging up their coats. Instead of taking the time to be fully present and learn more about them, I was focusing on my insecurity. Have you ever observed yourself acting like a crazy person, coupled with the urgency to tell yourself to pull it together? I circled each guest maniacally, repeating, "I just want you to know this is not our home; it is only a rental." Overwhelmed and embarrassed, I kept saying, "This is not my home!" In shame, I sequestered myself all night in the kitchen, missing meaningful opportunities to connect with God's people. Later that evening, after everyone had left and I was washing the dishes, I began replaying the picture of a hysterical pastor's wife saying, "This is not my home!" With my hands submerged in the warm soapy water, the Holy Spirit gently convicted my heart. *Karen, dear child, that was the most truthful thing you said all evening. This rental, this world is not your home; you are a citizen of Heaven. You are called to be a holy pilgrim who is just passing through this world.* I did not realize it at the time, but I enrolled in pilgrim school that night. My kitchen sink was hallowed ground.

Holy Presence

The first home was perfect. It was a garden filled with beauty and everything man and woman could ever want. Their relationship with one another and God was perfectly united. They lived naked and unashamed. Man and woman walked in His presence in the cool of the day. When sin entered the world, this home was broken. They hid from God, and in their shame, they sought to cover their sin with flimsy fig leaves. In love, God pursued them, and through the shedding of blood, He covered their nakedness with animal skins. Sin brought separation, but their Savior provided a way for them to live in His presence. He promised One would come and crush the enemy's head, providing a way to live in the Father's presence. Now Adam and Eve would have loved to settle securely in the garden forever, but their sin forced them to leave it and become pilgrims.

The children of Israel were fellow wanderers. For forty years, they walked around the sandy wilderness. God looked down and saw a stiff-necked people whom He loved and desired to become holy and set apart. He occupied a portable house for them to camp around His presence. He instructed them to place the

Tabernacle tent in the center of the twelve tribes. Every family was to orient their lives around the Tent of Meeting. The glory cloud filled the Tabernacle, and His people worshiped their God. They longed to reach the Holy Land and be settlers, but for now they were called to be pilgrims. As pilgrims, they lived a transient life in tents. They pitched them in His presence. When the Tabernacle moved, they moved. God provided daily bread. A pillar of fire enlightened their pilgrim path by night and the glory cloud by day. God's presence was the distinguishing characteristic of His people over the decades. God delivered slaves who were settlers to become pilgrims who were free.

Solomon was instructed to build God a dwelling place. Detailed instructions were given for the elaborate construction of the Temple. This permanent home was to be the center of Jewish life. God's children were in awe as God's glory filled this place. God's perfect design for His building points to His detailed design for His body of believers. The standard was perfection, and it would not be possible without His presence. When the Temple was destroyed, the people of God longed for their house of worship to be rebuilt. Jesus came as Immanuel, God with us. The Word became flesh. He left His heavenly home and tabernacled, or pitched His tent, with His people. He would call twelve disciples to pilgrim alongside Him to spread His kingdom. They would be called to leave their homes and have no place to lay their heads. As we learned last week, as He faced the cross, He told them He was going to prepare a heavenly Home for them. He must lay down His life to provide a way for them to live in His presence forever. He prophesied even though the Jews would seek to tear down the Temple, He would rebuild it in three days. Jesus's perfect life, death, and resurrection provide the way to live in His presence.

As you and I pilgrim through this radical now-and-not-yet world, we have been given a Helper. The Spirit dwells within each follower of Christ. Our bodies were designed to be His temple. The Spirit comes alongside us on the pilgrim path when we are tempted to seek our own way. He convicts and counsels us when we are tempted to stop walking, to settle, and to pitch a tent around our sinful habits. He will guide and provide each step of the journey until we get Home. Jesus will return to take us there to live with Him. Heaven is the perfect dwelling place. It is a Home that is forever marked by His presence with His people.

Hallowed Be Your Name

Our daughter's name, Anna Grace, means "beautiful grace." It was our prayer that her life might be a living portrait of the beautiful grace of God to her and others. Throughout the Bible, we see a name is more than something you are called; it encompasses your whole being. Back to our pilgrim Moses, when called to take his first steps to lead the pilgrimage out of Egypt, he felt he lacked a proper name for God. God introduced Himself to Moses as simply the God of your fathers (Ex. 3:6). He needed a name for God equal to the mission he was being called to fulfill. He believed knowing the name would bring the credibility of His character to questioning followers. Moses knew he needed a trustworthy answer when the people would ask the name of the person who was sending them out into the desert, ". . . and they ask me, 'What is His name?' What shall I say to them?" God said to Moses, "I am who I am" (Ex. 3:13-14). "Yahweh" sums up all of who God is in His character and reputation and all of what He can do in His authority and power. "Holy and awesome is His name" (Ps. 111:9)!

God's people also needed His law to learn to live in His presence. Moses summited a mountain to receive God's laws carved into two pieces of stone. One of those ten commandments instructs His followers to keep His name holy (Ex. 20:7). As he descended the heights, Moses was still on a mission to deliver the children of Israel to the promised land. He was weary and ready to quit. The journey had been long, and the people had been difficult. He pleaded with God for the promise of His presence. God replied, "My presence will go with you, and I will give you rest" (Ex. 33:14). God's presence is another way of saying "His face."

God would go before and alongside Moses until they crossed the Jordan River. Their trajectory was the promised land. This home was "flowing with milk and honey" and would deliver them everlasting rest. The answer to this desperate prayer would also distinguish His children as they lived among a new people. Moses uttered the cry of every pilgrim leader, "Please show me Your glory" (Ex. 33:18). The LORD graciously placed him in the crack of a rock so he could catch a glimpse of His glory. God declared, "I will make all My goodness pass before you and will proclaim before you My name 'The LORD.' And I will be gracious to whom I will be gracious, and will show mercy on whom I will show mercy" (Ex. 33:19). God's glory is displayed in His attributes. With hallowing God's name, Moses encountered transformation into a radiantly set-apart man.

Holy, Holy, Holy! Lord God Almighty!

Holy, holy, holy! Lord God Almighty!
Early in the morning, my song shall rise to Thee.
Holy, holy, holy! Merciful and mighty!
God in three persons, blessed Trinity!

Holy, holy, holy! Though the darkness hide Thee,
Though the eyes of sinful man Thy glory may not see,
Only Thou art holy; there is none beside Thee
Perfect in power, in love, and purity.

Holy, holy, holy! Lord God Almighty!
All Thy works shall praise Thy name in earth and sky and sea.
Holy, holy, holy! Merciful and mighty!
God in three persons, blessed Trinity!

Reginald Heber[1]

Hallowed and Holy Are We

Like Moses, we cannot encounter a holy God in our personal or corporate worship and leave unchanged. Isaiah set out on a prophet's pilgrimage and encountered a holy God. Worship overflows as he cried out, "Holy, holy, holy is the Lord of hosts; the whole earth is full of His glory" (Isa. 6:3)! He looked up in wonder and looked within and was undone. Open-handed worship yields open-hearted surrender. He was a man on a mission, "Here am I send me" (Isa. 6:8).

Mary, the mother of Jesus, was overwhelmed when the angel delivered the news: she is pregnant with the Son of God. Her response is filled with faith and surrender. "For nothing will be impossible with God. Behold, I am the servant of the Lord; let it be to me according to your word" (Luke 1:37-38). Her pilgrimage to parenthood would not be what she expected, and yet the overflow of her heart was worship: "My soul magnifies the Lord, and my spirit rejoices in God my Savior" (Luke 1:46-47). Worship and surrender are the supernatural response to hallowing God's name. Their postures are the same—open-handed. Pilgrims yield to the Spirit and seek to live open-handed and open-hearted. Their hearts extend upward in worship, and their feet walk by faith and not by sight.

To hallow something means to set it apart as holy or different. Throughout Scripture, God sets things apart. There was the tree of the knowledge of good and evil in the garden, and the Sabbath as a day to rest from work and rest unto Him. Sacrificial offerings were divided between clean and unclean in Leviticus, and the Holy of Holies for the priests in the Temple. We hallow God's name by not profaning or taking it in vain. We also hallow it as our lives are set apart in a corrosive culture. People will observe we are different when there is little gap between public and private worship. We will radiate His glory as we seek to image His attributes.

Hallowing His name is the juncture where our theology and doxology converge. *Theology* is a word or thought about God. *Doxology* is a word or thought about glory. Our theology and doxology compel us to worship and surrender. When we pray to hallow His name, we ask God to cleanse and purify our lives, words, emotions, choices, and relationships. We cannot make God's name more holy, but we can seek to reverence it as more holy in our daily lives. This holy transformation requires total surrender, "present your bodies as a living sacrifice, holy and acceptable to God, which is your spiritual worship" (Rom. 12:1). Holy worship yields radical surrender. Renewal of our minds happens when His Word does His sanctifying work in our lives. Our faces will radiate God's glory to a watching world as we are changed. Yet our faces are not veiled like Moses', "And we all, with unveiled face, beholding the glory of the Lord, are being transformed into the same image from one degree of glory to another. For this comes from the Lord who is the Spirit" (2 Cor. 3:18).

> We are products of our theology and our doxology. What we believe about God and what we esteem and elevate as praiseworthy will profoundly shape our lives. Our theology and doxology are inseparably connected.
>
> Karen Hodge and Susan Hunt [2]

The more times I have moved, the more I have purged. And yet I am always astonished by the sheer accumulation of stuff. The reality is I am more of a settler than a pilgrim. Pilgrims are called to travel light while settlers are burdened by the cares of this world. Pilgrims have forward momentum, while settlers are often stuck and stagnant. Pilgrims' lives are centered on eternal matters, while settlers are focused on temporal things. A settler is tethered to this earth while a pilgrim is just passing through. Pilgrims look up in worship and step out in surrender. Settlers are myopic and look inward to sinful and selfish desires. The difference in perspectives between pilgrims and settlers has everything to do with where they fix their eyes. A pilgrim directs her prayers heavenward with each step along the journey. Pilgrims seek to remove "every sin which clings so closely and run with endurance the race that is set before us, looking to Jesus, the founder, and perfecter of our faith" (Heb.12:1b-2). A pilgrim asks the Spirit to make His home in her life in such a way she hallows His name in every part of her life. We cannot hallow His name until He hallows us first.

Weekly Prayer List

Write the Lord's Prayer over your life this week. Spend time writing out your prayer requests in these four areas. Come back to this list daily to continue to ask, seek, or knock. Put a star next to answered prayers. And then on day seven, reflect and praise God for what He has done and allow the remaining items to shape your prayers for next week.

Our Father in heaven, hallowed be Your name. Your kingdom come, Your will be done, on earth as it is in heaven. Give us this day our daily bread, and forgive us our debts, as we also have forgiven our debtors. And lead us not into temptation, but deliver us from evil (Matt. 6:9-13).

Personal Prayer

Family Prayer

Church Prayer

Prayer for my neighbors (work or community)

Day One: Pilgrim Pathway

INHALE GOD'S WORD

Having a pilgrim's perspective rather than a settler's perspective has everything to do with where we fix our eyes. Consider the following contrasts between living as a pilgrim and a settler. Write examples of how you have seen yourself living more like a settler than a pilgrim.

Pilgrim's Perspective	Heavenly minded Forward moving and strategic Travels light Full of faith Worshipper of God Surrendered to His will
Settler's Perspective	Earth-bound thinking Stopped & stagnant Burdened by the world Filled with fear Worshipper of self Reluctant to obey
Personal Examples	

EXHALE IN PRAYER ~ ADORATION

Dear Father, I worship because You are holy, holy, holy . . .

GO BACK TO YOUR WEEKLY PRAYER LIST AND SPEND TIME IN PRAYER.

Day Two: Heaven Is Our Home

Our trajectory towards Home has everything to do with where we fix our eyes. Spend time in these passages and note where our eyes need to be focused.

INHALE GOD'S WORD

Passage	Focus
Psalm 121	
2 Corinthians 4:16-18	
Hebrews 12:1-2	
Revelation 21:1-7	

EXHALE IN PRAYER ~ ADORATION

Dear Father, I lift my eyes to You and worship You because. . .

GO BACK TO YOUR WEEKLY PRAYER LIST AND SPEND TIME IN PRAYER.

Day Three: Prayer Book – The Psalms

INHALE GOD'S WORD

Read Psalm 51. On the top of the box write the words from this psalm which describe the greatness and goodness of God. On the bottom half of this box write the words which describe man's need and the nature of his sin.

GOD

MAN

EXHALE IN PRAYER ~ CONFESSION

Dear Father, create in me a clean heart and renew a right spirit within me by . . .

GO BACK TO YOUR WEEKLY PRAYER LIST AND SPEND TIME IN PRAYER.

Day Four: Hallowed Be Your Name

INHALE GOD'S WORD

Spend time reflecting on some of God's names in the Bible and then write next to each what hallowing it in your life will mean for you this week.

Elohim—Creator (Gen. 1:1)____

El Elyon—Most High God (Ps. 57:2)__________________________________

El Roi—God Who Sees (Gen. 16:13)__________________________________

El Shaddai—LORD Almighty (Gen. 17:1)_______________________________

Adonai—LORD and Master (Ps. 40:17)_________________________________

Jehovah—I AM (Ex. 3:14)____

Jehovah Jireh—God Who Provides(Gen.22:14)____________________________

Jehovah Roi—LORD is my Shepherd (Ps. 23)_____________________________

EXHALE IN PRAYER ~ CONFESSION

Dear Father, I confess I look to others for help rather than running to You for . . .

GO BACK TO YOUR WEEKLY PRAYER LIST AND SPEND TIME IN PRAYER.

Day Five: Hallowed Be Your Name

INHALE GOD'S WORD

Today spend time reflecting on these passages which outline God's incommunicable and communicable attributes.

Incommunicable Attributes - Attributes only God possesses

Attribute	Definition	Passage
Self-existent	Not created	Isaiah 41:4; 42:8
Eternality	Always existed	Genesis 21:33; Exodus 3:14
Immutability	Cannot change	Psalm 102:26-27; Numbers 23:19
Omniscience	All-knowing	Psalm 139:1-6; Matthew 6:8
Omnipresence	All-present	Psalm 139:7-12; Jeremiah 23:23
Omnipotent	All-powerful	Psalm 139:13-16; Isaiah 13:6

Communicable Attributes - Attributes that God and man, by God's grace, possess

Attribute	Definition	Passage
Holiness	Set apart	Isaiah 6:3; Psalm 77:13
Righteousness	Right standing	Psalm119:137; 145:17
Truthfulness	Cannot lie	Numbers 23:19; Hebrews 10:23
Love	Self-sacrificial	1 John 4:8; Romans 5:8
Goodness	Benevolent	Exodus 34:6-7; Jeremiah 31:3
Mercy	Kind to the needy	Psalm 86:15; Luke 6:36

EXHALE IN PRAYER ~ THANKSGIVING

Dear Father, I thank You for each of these attributes . . .

GO BACK TO YOUR WEEKLY PRAYER LIST AND SPEND TIME IN PRAYER.

Day Six: Hallow Me

INHALE GOD'S WORD

Read and reflect on the Scripture proofs from the *Westminster Shorter Catechism*, Questions #100 and 101.[3]

Q. 100: What does the preface of the Lord's Prayer teach us?

A: The preface of the Lord's Prayer (which is, *Our Father in heaven*) teaches us firstly to draw near to God with all holy reverence (Ps. 95:6) and confidence (Eph. 3:12) as children to a father (Rom. 8:15) able and ready to help us (Eph. 3:20); and secondly, that we should pray with and for others (1 Tim. 2:1-2).

Q. 101: What do we pray for in the first request?

A: In the first request (which is, *Hallowed be Your name*) we pray that God may enable us and others to glorify Him in all in which He makes Himself known (Ps. 67:1-3; Ps. 100:3-4); and that He would overrule all things for His own glory (Rom. 11:33-36; Rev. 4:11).

EXHALE IN PRAYER ~ THANKSGIVING

Dear Father, I thank You that You love me enough to hallow my words, actions, attitudes, and relationships this week by. . .

GO BACK TO YOUR WEEKLY PRAYER LIST AND SPEND TIME IN PRAYER.

Day Seven: Write His Prayer over Your Life

INHALE GOD'S WORD

Read back through our passage for this week: Matthew 6:9b.

What are three takeaways that you learned this week through your personal study, prayer journaling, or your small group discussion?

1.

2.

3.

EXHALE IN PRAYER ~ SUPPLICATION

Dear Father, would You give me faith to live these truths out this week by . . .

RETURN TO YOUR WEEKLY PRAYER LIST

- Place a star next to answered prayers.
- Spend time giving praise to God.
- Reflect upon His persevering grace for what remains on your prayer list.
- Ask God to apply what you have learned this week as you seek His face to write your prayer list for next week.

---

1 Reginald Heber, "Holy, Holy, Holy!" in *Trinity Hymnal* (Suwanee, GA: Great Commission Publications, 2021), 100.

2 Karen Hodge and Susan Hunt, *Transformed, Life-taker to Life-giver* (Geanies House, Scotland: Christian Focus Publications, 2016), 7.

3 *The Westminster Shorter Catechism* (Lawrenceville GA: Committee on Discipleship Ministries, 1990), 31.

Week Four:

Priority

Learning to pray as a Loyal Steward

Matthew 6:10

Teaching
WEEKLY FOCUS & IDENTITY THEMES

Matthew 6:10

Your kingdom come, Your will be done, on earth as it is in heaven.

Along my Christian pilgrimage, I have reached many crossroads. Should I go left or right, choose easy or hard, say yes or no? Sometimes the decisions are complex, and other times they are easy. Looking back along these paths, I now see there was a greater implication of obedience at play. In these crucibles of decision-making, we can either pride ourselves we are in control or despair over the fact we have lost control. Both are laughable. Whether it is who we will marry, what career we will choose, or whether we will seek the good of others or ourselves on a hard Monday, the ultimate question is not what will happen, but rather who is the sovereign ruler of my life? Who or what have I enthroned in my heart? This choice will reveal whether I seek to build my own little kingdom or pray for His kingdom to come. As I wrestle over what to do, the ultimate question will be answered—my will or His will be done? The more we seek to hallow His name, the more we are compelled to bend the knee to the sovereign King of the universe. We are not our own; we are called to be His loyal stewards. Praying "Your kingdom come, Your will be done on earth as it is in heaven" is not a safe prayer. It holds within it the power to change everything.

Rule

A king seated on the throne both rules and reigns. Ruling is all about exercising authority, control, and dominion. We may fancy ourselves as little despots claiming ultimate authority and power over our lives, but when life around us begins to unravel or crumble, we cry out in fear when others are out to overthrow our little kingdom. Who or what we esteem as the sovereign ruler or authority in our lives shapes everything we say and do. When self is on the throne, the needs of others are secondary. When feelings dominate, our lives are unstable and insecure. When the world's values are preeminent, the Word is forgotten. God must be our reference point for all of life, and His Word is our ultimate authority. Daily we are called to repent and to seek by faith to dethrone these lesser rulers relentlessly. We often live like the children of Israel in the days of the Judges, ". . . there was no king in Israel. Everyone did what was right in his own eyes" (Judg. 21:25).

Crown Him With Many Crowns

Crown Him with many crowns,
The Lamb upon His throne;
Hark! how the heavenly anthem drowns
All music but its own:
Awake, my soul, and sing
Of Him who died for thee,
And hail Him as thy matchless King
Through all eternity.

Crown Him the Lord of love;
 Behold His hands and side,
Rich wounds, yet visible above,
 In beauty glorified:
 No angel in the sky
 Can fully bear that sight,
But downward bends his burning eye
 At mysteries so bright.

Crown Him the Lord of peace;
 Whose power a scepter sways
From pole to pole, that wars may cease,
 Absorbed in prayer and praise:
 His reign shall know no end;
 And round His pierced feet
Fair flowers of paradise extend
 Their fragrance ever sweet.

Crown Him the Lord of years,
 The Potentate of time;
Creator of the rolling spheres,
 Ineffably sublime:
 All hail, Redeemer, hail!
 For Thou hast died for me:
Thy praise shall never, never fail
 Throughout eternity.

Matthew Bridges (1851)[1]

Reign

Who is this King of glory? The LORD of hosts, He is the King of glory (Ps. 24:10)!

The Garden of Eden is our first glance at the Kingdom of God. There was beauty, peace, order, and perfect obedience to the King's will. Man and woman as well as all of creation flourished. In the Fall, they discarded the authority of God's Word and will. Rather than serving the King, they sought to serve themselves. Sin entered the world as man and woman declared self-sovereignty. Throughout the Old Testament fallen men would look to fallen rulers to restore the beauty, peace, and the order they craved. There were many kings and rulers, some were good and others were evil. There was even a king after God's own heart named David, but even he was not the perfect king. We needed a new and better king. So, God in His mercy established a covenant with David which promised One who would rule and reign forever. "When your days are fulfilled and you lie down with your fathers, I will raise up your offspring after you, who shall come from your body, and I will establish his kingdom. He shall build a house for My name, and I will establish the throne of his kingdom forever. I will be to him a father, and he shall be to Me a son" (2 Sam. 7:12-14).

The angel Gabriel announced to Mary her son would be the long-awaited King in the Davidic line. "He will be great and will be called the Son of the Most High. And the Lord God will give to Him the throne of His father David" (Luke 1:32). The King arrived and was not placed on a royal throne but rather in a manger. Jesus's rule and reign brought the hope of ultimate beauty, peace, and order, but it would be a deferred kingdom as He continually demonstrated, "My kingdom is not of this world" (John 18:36). In the most epic role reversal, the King became the servant on the cross. "For even the Son of Man came not to be served but to serve, and to give His life as a ransom for many" (Mark 10:45). Jesus also said, ". . . the kingdom of God is near" (Luke 21:31). So, the kingdom of God has come, but it has not achieved its most extensive rule and reign. It is an already-but-not-yet kingdom. God appointed Christ as ruler over all things. He is a kind and benevolent king who is ruling and reigning on high for the benefit of us—the Church— "that He worked in Christ when He raised Him from the dead and seated Him at His right hand in the heavenly places, far above all rule and authority and power and dominion, and above every name that is named, not only in this age but also in the one to come. And He put all things under His feet and gave Him as head over all things to the church" (Eph. 1:20-22). Until King Jesus returns, He is actively gathering and sanctifying kingdom citizens (Phil. 3:20). God promises when Jesus returns in His royal glory, "every knee should bow, in heaven and on earth and under the earth, and every tongue confess that Jesus Christ is Lord, to the glory of God the Father" (Phil. 2:10-11). We live among people who long for beauty, peace, and order. They look inward and outward to find these virtues from a sustainable source. May we live our lives with unquestioned allegiance and crown Him "Lord of all" in such a way that the world might lean and look and ask, "Who is this King of glory?"

His Kingdom Come

From before the foundation of the world until He comes again, Jesus is the uncontested and unrivaled King of kings. The critical question is, do I live as though He is the uncontested or unrivaled sovereign of my life? He is a jealous ruler, and there is no room for rivals. The Ten Commandments begin with, "You shall have no other gods before Me" (Ex. 20:3). When we pray "Your kingdom come," it's an imperative command rooted in the indicative of His divine kingship. The Kingdom of God is the realm where God is acknowledged as King in the hearts of obedient stewards. As we pray these powerful petitions corporately, we affirm our allegiance to His sovereign rule. We are asking our Father to extend His rule and reign in three specific arenas.

First, we pray for His kingdom to come ultimately—for the establishment of His eternal kingdom when all creation will acknowledge Him as King of kings and Lord of lords. This petition echoes the final prayer of the Bible: "He who testifies to these things says, 'Surely I am coming soon.' Amen. Come, Lord Jesus!" (Rev. 22:20). Secondly, we pray for His kingdom to come globally. We ask for the light of the gospel to spread to the ends of the earth. We pray God's rule might be displayed to others through us as we "Go therefore and make disciples of all nations, baptizing them in the name of the Father and of the Son and of the Holy Spirit, teaching them to observe all that I have commanded you. And behold, I am with you always, to the end of the age" (Matt. 28:19-20). Finally, we pray His kingdom might come inwardly as His rule and reign extend to every fiber of our being. The kingdom has to come in our hearts before we can be agents of change in His kingdom. Remember, this is a dangerous prayer to pray. As God answers this prayer, you and I will be nothing less than transformed.

Here are a few diagnostic questions we can ask ourselves to reveal whether there are rivals to the throne of our hearts.

- What do you treasure?
- What, if you were threatened to lose it, would make you angry?
- What makes you anxious when things are unknown?
- What motivates you?
- What gives you the greatest joy?
- What gives you the most frustration when it seems like things are out of control?
- How are these things ruling and reigning in your heart?

There is no room in His kingdom for divided allegiance, "no one can serve two masters" (Matt. 6:24). When His kingdom comes, our lives and faith move from being bifurcated to integrated. Mark begins his Gospel with our daily call to obedience to this prayer, ". . . the kingdom of God is at hand; repent and believe in the gospel" (Mark 1:15). Jesus challenges us to "seek first the kingdom of God and His righteousness, and all these things will be added to you" (Matt. 6:33). May God give us grace to be unrelenting to dethrone self and enthrone the King.

> Three doctrinal statements bring the Lord's Prayer together. The first two come in the invocation. God is the Father of Christian people, and He is in heaven. The third rounds off the first trio of petitions: in heaven God's will is done. The first proclaims God's goodness in redeeming us through the cross and taking us into His family. The second and third declare His greatness and power to achieve His purpose. Together, these three truths point up the Christian's hope. As our Father, God stands pledged to love us and do us good for all eternity.
>
> J.I. Packer[2]

Stewardship

Back to solving my little life conundrums. Why do I fret so? It can be boiled down to whether I view my life in terms of ownership or stewardship. If you had grown up in the Hodge household, you would have heard this phrase repeatedly: "All of life is stewardship!" Our family has always thought of our calling to be stewards, defined as something of inestimable value entrusted by the King for kingdom purposes. What has been entrusted? His Word, His people, and all of creation. Individually He has entrusted us with gifts and graces, time, and resources to be invested for His glory.

Jesus shared a stewardship parable with His disciples in Matthew 25:14-30. The master did not have to give talents, but graciously "to one he gave five talents, to another two, to another one, to each according to his ability" (Matt. 25:15). These are gifts entrusted for kingdom purposes. The servant who received one talent chose fear and hoarding over stewardship. The master responded, "You wicked and slothful servant!" (Matt. 25:26). Those who were given two and five talents were loyal stewards. They doubled their initial kingdom investment and received the commendation of the master, "Well done, good and faithful servant. You have been faithful over a little; I will set you over much. Enter into the joy of your master" (Matt. 25:23). Stewards seek to invest in eternal things which will promote His kingdom extension and His will being done.

There is not a square inch in the whole domain of our human existence over which Christ, who is Sovereign over all, does not cry, "Mine!"

Abraham Kuyper[3]

The blueprint for being a loyal steward of the King is spelled at the beginning, "So, God created man in His own image, in the image of God He created him; male and female He created them. And God blessed them. And God said to them, 'Be fruitful and multiply and fill the earth and subdue it, and have dominion'" (Gen. 1:27-28). God is the King, and we are His vice-regents. In the ancient world, kings would erect statues or seal documents with their image to establish the borders of their reign. Our kingdom purpose is to be sent out as His image-bearers to embody the mission of the King. He sends us out to spread the fame of His name to the ends of the earth. The King bestows His authority on us as He gives us dominion to cultivate and keep His creation, but never for us and our controlling purposes. As stewards we declare to a watching world everything belongs to Him. Faithful stewardship hallows Him as the preeminent Creator King. "For by Him all things were created, in heaven and on earth, visible and invisible, whether thrones or dominions or rulers or authorities—all things were created through Him and for Him. And He is before all things, and in Him all things hold together. And He is the head of the body, the church. He is the beginning, the firstborn from the dead, that in everything He might be preeminent" (Col. 1:16-18).

His Will Be Done on Earth as It Is in Heaven

In heaven the King is on the throne, and the angels obey His will perfectly. The most remarkable example of His Father's will being "done on earth as it is in heaven" was modeled by Jesus in the Garden of Gethsemane. How did Jesus discover God's will? He knelt and prayed. Matthew 26:36-46 records that although Jesus always perfectly fulfilled the will of His Father, He wrestled over the cost of obedience. The cup was costly. When He went to the cross, He had to drink the cup of God's wrath—for your sin and mine—to the bitter dregs bearing the full weight of God's holy fury against sin. He was separated from His Father's fellowship which He had experienced from eternity past. He was betrayed, tried, convicted, mocked, beaten, and executed. Yet through all this, God's will was done perfectly. "And going a little farther He fell on His face and prayed, saying, 'My Father, if it be possible, let this cup pass from Me; nevertheless, not as I will, but as You will'" (Matt. 26:39).

Perhaps you wonder, how could this have been God's will? His Word tells us the cross was no mistake. "Yet it was the will of the LORD to crush Him; He has put Him to grief; when His soul makes an offering for guilt, He shall see His offspring; He shall prolong His days; the will of the LORD shall prosper in His hand" (Isa. 53:10).

Kingdom Praying

King Jesus, rule supreme in my life.
King Jesus, dominate my thoughts.
King Jesus, reign over every member of my body.
King Jesus, exercise full sovereignty over me.
King Jesus, let Your will be the preoccupation of my life.

Michael Youssef[4]

Surrender

If you have ever wrestled with doing God's will, you are not alone; Jesus did too. If we can't say "Your will be done" from the bottom of our hearts, we will never know peace, beauty, and order. Instead, we will feel compelled to control people and our environment by manipulating them according to our purposes. The world boasts that seeking control and authority brings freedom. The King tells us that seeking ultimate authority and control never brings freedom. Surrender on our knees to His will being done brings freedom.

Finding God's will is not a problem to be solved but a privilege to be stewarded.

Aimee Joseph[5]

If we want to know God's will, we must give our lives to know His Word. Our minds must be transformed to discern His will. "Do not be conformed to this world but be transformed by the renewal of your mind, that by testing you may discern what is the will of God, what is good and acceptable and perfect" (Rom. 12:2). Sometimes we may be overly distracted seeking to discern God's sovereign secret will rather than beginning with focus on God's written revealed will.

It is His revealed will for us to be adopted into His family (Eph. 1:5). It is His will for us to do good to others (1 Peter 2:15). God's will is accomplished when we give thanks in all circumstances (1 Thess. 5:18). And our sanctification is God's will (1 Thess. 4:3). We are sanctified and hallowed as we obey His revealed will. We understand God's will as we walk it out "by faith, not by sight" (2 Cor. 5:7). Sometimes we discover aspects of His secret sovereign will as we look at our lives in the rearview mirror. At other times, for His glory, it will remain hidden, but that does not negate the fact He "works all things according to the counsel of His will" (Eph. 1:11). And when we finally get Home, we will understand and obey His will perfectly.

Decision-making often causes us to expend a lot of emotional energy seeking one right choice. It is a game-changer to consider discerning the will of God as a privilege to be stewarded. He has entrusted us with the privilege of walking His will in the context of relationship with Him and others. Along this path, His will for us unfolds—our sanctification. Each choice and its decision have the potential to either conform us to the world or transform us by His Word. One of the primary purposes of prayer is to grow us into mature and loyal stewards, not seeking to bend God's will to us, but to mold our will into His.

Maybe you, too, are facing some big decisions along your Christian pilgrimage. As a gospel-friend, I want to tell you, there is always a yield sign at each choice-crossroad. To yield is to acquiesce, submit, or surrender. When driving, yielding allows another car to go in front of us. For the believer the will of the steward should be rightly subordinated to the will of the Sovereign. This is the hallowed intersection where we bow the knee and open our hands and heart, ready and receptive to follow the will of the King. The directional signs at this crossroad read "Thy will" or "My will." We stand at this daily discipleship juncture and are called to deny ourselves. As He said to all, "If anyone would come after Me, let him deny himself and take up his cross daily and follow Me" (Luke 9:23). This is where rivals to His rule and reign must be crucified, whether they are our plans, agendas, or visions of self-glory. But we do not travel this path alone. Christ invites us to come, learn, and be yoked as we follow His lead. "Take My yoke upon you, and learn from Me, for I am gentle and lowly in heart, and you will find rest for your souls. For My yoke is easy, and My burden is light" (Matt. 11:29-30). When we walk the path of God's will, each step leads us to worship Him as the uncontested and unrivaled Sovereign over our lives. It is the King's delight to enable each step for His kingdom to come more extensively and His will to be done more gloriously in and through our lives.

Weekly Prayer List

Write the Lord's Prayer over your life this week. Spend time writing out your prayer requests in these four areas. Come back to this list daily to continue to ask, seek, or knock. Put a star next to answered prayers. And then on day seven, reflect and praise God for what He has done and allow the remaining items to shape your prayers for next week.

Our Father in heaven, hallowed be Your name. Your kingdom come, Your will be done, on earth as it is in heaven. Give us this day our daily bread, and forgive us our debts, as we also have forgiven our debtors. And lead us not into temptation, but deliver us from evil (Matt. 6:9-13).

Personal Prayer

Family Prayer

Church Prayer

Prayer for my neighbors (work or community)

Day One: Rule

INHALE GOD'S WORD

Take some time to read the following scriptures and reflect on these heart-diagnostic questions to determine what is ruling and reigning in your heart.

Read Matthew 13:44-46, Philippians 4:11-13, Galatians 2:20, Luke 9:23-27.

What do you treasure?

What, if you were threatened to lose it, would make you angry?

What makes you anxious when things are unknown?

What motivates you?

What gives you the greatest joy?

What gives you the most frustration when it seems like things are out of control?

How are these things ruling and reigning in your heart?

EXHALE IN PRAYER ~ ADORATION

Dear King of kings, I praise You for these glorious and wondrous works I have seen this week . . .

GO BACK TO YOUR WEEKLY PRAYER LIST AND SPEND TIME IN PRAYER.

Day Two: Prayer Book – The Psalms

INHALE GOD'S WORD

Who is the King of glory? Read Psalm 24 and write the attributes and actions of the King in the crown.

Let's make it personal.

Crown Him with many crowns!
Crown Him the Lord of love.
Crown Him the Lord of peace.
Crown Him the Lord of years.

Who is the King of glory to you personally?

Do your words and actions communicate in such a way so the world leans in and asks, "Who is the King of glory?"

Go back to page 58 and sing through this hymn and make it a prayer to the Lord.

EXHALE IN PRAYER ~ ADORATION

Dear King of glory, I praise You for how strong and mighty You are on my behalf...

GO BACK TO YOUR WEEKLY PRAYER LIST AND SPEND TIME IN PRAYER.

Day Three: Kingdom Come & His Will Be Done

INHALE GOD'S WORD

Read and reflect on Questions #123 and 124 from the *Heidelberg Catechism*.[6] Circle key scriptures that help you better understand how to pray for His kingdom to come and His will to be done.

Q. 123: What does the second petition mean?

A: "Your kingdom come" means: Rule us by Your Word and Spirit in such a way that more and more we submit to You (Ps. 119:5, 105; 143:10; Matt. 6:33). Preserve Your church and make it grow (Ps.122:6-9; Matt.16:18; Acts 2:42-47). Destroy the devil's work; destroy every force which revolts against You and every conspiracy against Your holy Word (Rom. 16:20; 1 John 3:8). Do this until Your kingdom fully comes, when You will be all in all (Rom. 8:22-23; 1 Cor. 15:28; Rev. 22:17, 20).

Q. 124: What does the third petition mean?

A: "Your will be done, on earth as it is in heaven" means: Help us and all people to reject our own wills and to obey Your will without any back talk. Your will alone is good (Matt. 7:21; 16:24-26; Luke 22:42; Rom. 12:1-2; Titus 2:11-12). Help us one and all to carry out the work we are called to (1 Cor. 7:17-24; Eph. 6:5-9), as willingly and faithfully as the angels in heaven (Ps. 103:20-21).

EXHALE IN PRAYER ~ CONFESSION

Dear King of glory, forgive me for the following ways I have sought to be the sovereign of my life this week . . .

GO BACK TO YOUR WEEKLY PRAYER LIST AND SPEND TIME IN PRAYER.

Day Four: His Kingdom Come & His Will Be Done

INHALE GOD'S WORD

Read the passage and write a description.
Consider a decision you need to make this week. Write how it would look for . . .

His will to be done, informed by God's Word. Psalm 119:33-37

His will to be done willingly. John 15:1-16

His will to be done joyfully. Hebrews 12:1-3

EXHALE IN PRAYER ~ CONFESSION

Dear Ruler over my life, I repent of seeking my will over Your will in the following ways this week . . .

GO BACK TO YOUR WEEKLY PRAYER LIST AND SPEND TIME IN PRAYER.

Day Four: Stewardship

INHALE GOD'S WORD

Read Romans 11:33-36, Colossians 1:15-20, and Colossians 3:23-24.

Remember, our calling to be a loyal steward is something of inestimable value entrusted by the King for kingdom purposes. So, let's do an inventory for investment's sake. What has the King entrusted to you in your head, heart, and hands? Then, write one way you can invest from each category this week.

HEAD	HEART	HANDS
Your thoughts, ideas, opinions, plans, etc.	Your affections, compassion, relationships, etc.	Your gifts, graces, physical belongings, finances, etc.
INVESTMENT	INVESTMENT	INVESTMENT

EXHALE IN PRAYER ~ THANKSGIVING

Dear Sovereign Creator, thank You for all these things You have entrusted to me. Enable me to be a loyal and faithful steward this week in the following ways . . .

GO BACK TO YOUR WEEKLY PRAYER LIST AND SPEND TIME IN PRAYER.

Day Six: Surrender

INHALE GOD'S WORD

Take time to kneel with Christ in the Garden of Gethsemane. Read Matthew 26:36-46.
Now reflect on what you will face tomorrow:

Is there an area of your heart that needs to be crucified?

Is there something He is asking you to deny or a cross He is asking you to take up?

Are you wrestling by faith between His will or your will being done?

EXHALE IN PRAYER ~ THANKSGIVING

Dear Supreme Ruler, I thank You for Your Word and how it has informed me of Your will in this way . . .

GO BACK TO YOUR WEEKLY PRAYER LIST AND SPEND TIME IN PRAYER.

Day Seven: Writing His Prayer over Your Life

INHALE GOD'S WORD

Read back through our passage for this week, Matthew 6:10.
What are three takeaways you learned this week through your personal study, prayer journaling, or your small group discussion?

1.

2.

3.

EXHALE IN PRAYER ~ SUPPLICATION

Dear King of kings and Lord of lords, would You write Your prayer over my life, family, church, and neighbors. . .

RETURN TO YOUR WEEKLY PRAYER LIST

- Place a star next to answered prayers.
- Spend time giving praise to God.
- Reflect upon His persevering grace for what remains on your prayer list.
- Ask God to apply what you have learned this week as you seek His face to write your prayer list for next week.

1 Matthew Bridges and George Elvey, "Crown Him with Many Crowns" in *Trinity Hymnal* (Suwanee, GA: Great Commission Publications, 2021), 295.

2 J.I. Packer, *Praying the Lord's Prayer* (Wheaton, IL: Crossway, 2007), 65.

3 Quote from Abraham Kuyper's inaugural address at the dedication of the Free University. Found in *Abraham Kuyper: A Centennial Reader*, ed. James D. Bratt (Grand Rapids, MI: Eerdmans, 1998), 488.

4 Michael Youssef, *The Prayer That God Answers* (Nashville: Thomas Nelson, 2000), 84-85.

5 "Walking Each Other Home as We Discern Next Steps" with Aimee Joseph from *enCourage* Podcast, October 26, 2021, https://encourage.pcacdm.org/2021/10/26/e-154-with-aimee-joseph/

6 G.I. Williamson, *The Heidelberg Catechism: A Study Guide* (Phillipsburg, NJ: P&R Publishing, 1993), 217, 221.

Week Five:
Provision

Learning to pray as a Grateful Neighbor

Matthew 6:11

Teaching
WEEKLY FOCUS & IDENTITY THEMES

Matthew 6:11

Give us this day our daily bread,

Gratitude

Our seminary years in Birmingham, Alabama, were full of lean times and abundant learning. It was God's ordained gospel classroom where He taught me about dependence, contentment, anxiety, and generosity. We lived on my meager teacher salary while Chris attended seminary full time. Near Thanksgiving, I watched a TV commercial that appealed to the public to donate to needy families. It was a real tear-jerker until they panned to a shot of the woman opening her pantry. My tears turned to discontentment as I said, "She has more food than we do in our pantry!" The snare of the compare led to an evening full of discouragement and complaining. The following day, I opened my closet full of clothes, scarfed down breakfast from my pantry, and drove in my car to my inner-city classroom. Conviction washed over my heart as I spent the day with thirty first graders who had far less than I and yet exuded joy. The teacher became the pupil. I had much to learn about the richness of God's daily provision.

Jesus knew children are good teachers of contentment. He opened His arms wide and welcomed them. "Let the children come to Me; do not hinder them, for to such belongs the kingdom of God" (Mark 10:14). They never hesitated to believe Jesus was their generous Provider and Protector who opened His hands to give. They came dependent and needy with open hands to receive. When an honest dependency and lavish generosity converge, His kingdom comes and His will is done. This passage continues with a stark contrast as it introduces us to a rich yet discontented ruler. He began with a good question about what is needed to inherit eternal life. Then he flashed his spiritual resume of commandment-keeping. Jesus moved beyond earthly duty to the heart of the matter. He saw there was a territory of the kingdom that had not come in this man's heart. He told him, "You lack one thing: go, sell all that you have and give to the poor, and you will have treasure in heaven; and come, follow Me" (Mark 10:21). Jesus lifted the young man's eyes from the temporal riches to eternal treasures. Instead of responding as a dependent child, he departed a sad "independent" individual.

> For me, and for many of us, our first waking thought of the day is "I didn't get enough sleep." The next one is "I don't have enough time." Whether true or not, that thought of "not enough" occurs automatically before we even think to question or examine it. . . .This internal condition of scarcity, this mind set of scarcity, lives at the very heart of our jealousies, our greed, our prejudice, and our arguments with life. The opposite of scarcity is not abundance. It is enough.
>
> Brené Brown[1]

The ideology of scarcity is pervasive in our culture. "Not-enoughness" breeds discontentment and grumbling. A scarcity mindset fails to consider God's character. The default reaction is to hoard. Hoarding is the orientation of an orphan. We learned our first week how to pray as dependent daughters. Our Father is a generous Giver! He is ruling from heaven and is rich beyond our comprehension. He knows exactly what we need. He is the Source and the Sustainer for all our needs. "For from Him and through Him and to Him are all things. To Him be glory forever. Amen" (Rom. 11:36).

Prayer Pivot

> The first three petitions have expressed our primary commitment to our Father's reputation, rule, and plans as our Lord. The second three petitions express our humble reliance on Him as our Savior. We depend on the Father for His provision (of bread), pardon (of sins), and protection (from evil).
>
> Richard Coekin[2]

Our orientation determines the overflow of our hearts and lives. For years I have called myself a pipe for God. I am not a fancy copper pipe but a utilitarian PVC pipe you can find at Home Depot. A fancy name for this is a conduit—a channel to carry something from one place to another. Sin clogs our pipes. Repentance and faith keep our pipes free-flowing. It is important to note the prayer pivot this week. The first half of the Lord's Prayer is focused vertically on God's glory: His name, reign, kingdom, and will. The second half, which we begin this week, focuses horizontally on man's needs: his material, spiritual, and moral well-being. This prayer begins by lifting our eyes upward as we are comforted by our Father who is in heaven, and we stand in awe at the hallowing of His name. Then we kneel in surrender as we ask for His kingdom to come and His will to be done. From this humble posture, we shift our focus to inward and outward needs. At this moment, we see the glory gap. God is infinite, and we are finite. So, why does the Father graciously weave these dissimilar petitions together? God's glory is always to be preeminent over man's needs. But man is made to reflect God's glory. We can never be all God intended us to be until our lives are orientated around glorifying and enjoying Him. It is our chief end! His glory flows to us, and then as it flows through us, the overflow is to enjoy His Fatherly love as He provides, pardons, and protects—not just individually but corporately. God first, man second—that is the perfect order of prayer. His glory before our wants. "So, whether you eat or drink, or whatever you do, do all to the glory of God" (1 Cor. 10:31).

Give Us

During those seminary years, we also had the privilege to learn much about generosity. Frank and Barbara Barker, founders of Briarwood Presbyterian Church, were a spiritual father and mother to Chris and me. They cultivated a culture of generosity in every sphere they served. In their home, people feasted on physical and spiritual food. They were generous with their time to listen, pray, and shepherd us. They gave sacrificially of their resources to us and others. When I would fret over the perceived lack in our lives or the unknown of the future, they would gently remind me God has given grace sufficient for the moment. They often said, "You cannot borrow grace for tomorrow's troubles." Their lives and ministry were lived open-handed. They embodied the posture of a grateful neighbor. This culture of generosity spread wide and far and into our hearts. They shaped one of our family's purposes: Share fully, for all is the Lord's.

The Barkers also taught us how to feed large groups of people. We would help them weekly host men's prayer breakfasts and visitor dinners in their home. I was Barbara's "egg girl." She would send me into the living room to count the men and then tell me to crack an egg and half per man. She discipled me at her kitchen sink. I often lost track of the egg count, but no one ever went hungry. They fed large groups, but never five thousand.

The feeding of five thousand men, plus women and children, is recorded in all four Gospels. Hungry people need to be fed. A big need requires a big God. When faced with solving this dilemma, the disciples considered several options. They could send the people away, take up a collection, or take a quick inventory of available food. Man-made solutions would not meet this extreme need. Jesus teaches us to pray "give us," not "give me" daily bread. His prayer leaves no room for radical individualism. This gospel story showcases the orientation and the overflow that mark a generosity culture. God draws us near as He feeds His people. Feasting at the Father's table is an intimate thing. We must open our hands to receive His good gifts.

We see a little boy open his hands to share his lunch in this story. We see Jesus take the bread in His hands, lift it heavenward, give thanks, and then give it away. The disciples went from person to person, sharing God's provision to the masses. Not only were the people fed and satisfied, but the disciples had twelve baskets of food left over. This abundance was a tangible reminder for the disciples of God's provision. Notice in John's account, Jesus gave thanks. "Jesus then took the loaves, and when He had given thanks, He distributed them to those who were seated" (John 6:11). Jesus modeled an attitude of gratitude, and we can too as we give thanks before our meals. He reminds hungry people He alone is the Source for all that is good and needful.

Fear causes us to fret or hoard. Prayer and action always go hand in hand. Grateful neighbors are givers. They grab the hand of a brother or sister in Christ and are privileged to intercede on their behalf. We *get* to rather than *have* to be a conduit of God's blessing to others. We are humbled to "have something to share with anyone in need" (Eph. 4:28). Open-handed generosity was the gospel ethos that built the early Church. "And they devoted themselves to the apostles' teaching and the fellowship, to the breaking of bread and the prayers" (Acts 2:42).

The greatest commandment and the Lord's Prayer have the same orientation and overflow. "You shall love the Lord your God with all your heart and with all your soul and with all your strength and with all your mind, and your neighbor as yourself" (Luke 10:27). Hearts are oriented vertically toward loving God with our whole being. Then hands overflow horizontally as we seek to love our neighbor as we love ourselves. The more we seek to love God, the more we are compelled to love our neighbor. But the more devoted we are to loving our neighbors, the more quickly we come to the end of our compassion and are driven back to the love of the Father. One love fuels the other.

> This petition teaches us that we are to live our lives one day at a time . . . It doesn't say, "Lord give me my bread for this year, for this month, for this week." No, it's "this day" and "daily bread." When we realize that we're to live one day at a time and that this is the way God provides for our needs, we will begin to find satisfaction in life and will find anxiety disappearing.
>
> Spiros Zodhiates[3]

Daily Bread

Daily. Much has been written about this one little word in the Lord's Prayer, although this is the only time it occurs in the New Testament. *Bread* means more than a loaf. It encompasses our basic needs: food, shelter, companionship. It is everything necessary for the preservation of life. Every culture has bread. It might be a roll, loaf, or a tortilla. In the first century, bread had no preservatives, so it did not save beyond a day. *Daily bread* means all of God's provision for the coming day. Daily can be applied to the whole prayer. We pray God gives us a daily application and deeper appreciation of His Fatherhood, kingdom, will, provision, forgiveness, and protection. "Give us this day our daily bread" is a petition about daily dependence. It is actively trusting Him one day at a time. It is the difference between God providing necessities instead of luxuries. Truth be told, sometimes I want dessert more than I want bread. I tend to crave my "greeds" instead of humbly receiving my needs. God's gracious provision of daily bread is really a matter of life or death.

Even around a bountiful Thanksgiving table, we can only eat enough to last a day. Likewise, we cannot inhale enough air to last six months, much less six minutes. Spiritually we cannot hoard a storehouse of grace for our future needs. God never gives strength in advance. Our position as a grateful neighbor postures us in prayer as eager and expectant to receive His bounty. He is *Jehovah Jireh*, "The LORD will provide" (Gen. 22:14). We can be confident because we serve a God who will "supply every need of yours according to His riches in glory in Christ Jesus" (Phil. 4:19). "My grace is sufficient for you, for My power is made perfect in weakness" (2 Cor. 12:9). His grace is enough, yet we cry "not-enough!" His powerful provision is perfected in our neediness. The big question is do we see ourselves as utterly dependent or stubbornly independent? This is why "give us this day our daily bread" has to be an everyday request.

> We are told to ask for bread, as the Israelites were told to gather manna, on a day-to-day basis: the Christian way is to live in constant dependence on God, a day at a time. Also, we are to ask for the bread we need; i.e., for the supply of necessities, not luxuries we can do without. This petition does not sanctify greed.
>
> J.I. Packer[4]

> Believers do not pray to inform God about things unknown to Him, or urge Him to do His duty as though He were reluctant. On the contrary, they pray in order that they may arouse themselves to seek Him. To meditate on His promises, and to relieve themselves of their anxieties by pouring them into His bosom. By prayer they declare that from Him alone they hope and expect, both for themselves and for others, all good things.
>
> John Calvin[5]

Malnutrition

Back to our story of Jesus feeding the masses. The crowds were physically filled, but their hearts were still empty. The next day they came looking for another handout. They did not understand their deepest hunger was for significance, meaning, and purpose. We often look to bread that will never satisfy us. Christ went on to tell them He alone nourishes and satisfies. "I am the bread of life. Your fathers ate the manna in the wilderness, and they died. This is the bread that comes down from heaven, so that one may eat of it and not die. I am the living bread that came down from heaven. If anyone eats of this bread, he will live forever" (John 6:48-51). We need to whet our appetites for lasting nourishment. "Blessed are those who hunger and thirst for righteousness, for they shall be satisfied" (Matt. 5:6). He is a generous Father who gives us, "far more abundantly than all that we ask or think, according to the power at work within us, to Him be glory" (Eph. 3:20-21a).

The children of Israel were also enrolled in a gospel classroom with a contentment curriculum. The days were long, and the classroom was hot and sandy. They were hungry, stiff-necked, and grumbling students. Their stomachs were churning, but what they did not know was they needed more than their physical needs met; they were spiritually malnourished. How would Moses feed the masses? The LORD revealed to him that He would rain down bread from heaven. It was an extraordinary provision to meet an ordinary daily need. This class would also have a test. God wanted to see if His children would rely on Him for daily needs. Some followed the instructions, while others hoarded believing His provision was not enough. When morning came, the hoarded bread was full of maggots and began to smell. God was testing them to see if they would be obedient. Their daily dependence test was failed (Ex. 16:4-10, 17-20).

Discontentment robs us of the joy of being a grateful neighbor. We crave comfort and security. God provided what they had asked for, and yet they did not obey. They were trying to borrow grace for tomorrow. When we get more than we need, it tends to spoil. We are prone to wander and leave the God we love. Moses knew the children of Israel were also prone to forget, so he said, "Take a jar, and put an omer of manna in it, and place it before the LORD to be kept throughout your generations" (Ex. 16:33). They placed this portion in the ark of the covenant and carried it as they wandered through the desert.

Before God fed the children of Israel, He let them feel the pangs of hunger. He wanted their souls to feel their desperate need of Him. He was disciplining them to be dependent children. Moses explained God's lesson plans. "And He humbled you and let you hunger and fed you with manna, which you did not know, nor did your fathers know, that He might make you know that man does not live by bread alone, but man lives by every word that comes from the mouth of the LORD" (Deut. 8:3). Jesus quoted this passage after fasting forty days and forty nights—and He was hungry. The tempter came and said to Him, "If you are the Son of God, command these stones to become loaves of bread" (Matt. 4:3). God's Word provided the sustenance Jesus needed to fulfill His mission. His Word gave the children of Israel all they needed on their pilgrimage to the promised land. And His Word will also sustain you and me as we journey until we get Home.

Guide Me, O Thou Great Jehovah

Guide me, O Thou great Jehovah,
Pilgrim through this barren land;
I am weak, but Thou art mighty;
Hold me with Thy powerful hand;
Bread of heaven, Bread of heaven,
Feed me till I want no more,
Feed me till I want no more.

Open now the crystal fountain,
Whence the healing stream doth flow;
Let the fire and cloudy pillar
Lead me all my journey through;
Strong Deliverer, strong Deliverer,
Be Thou still my Strength and Shield,
Be Thou still my Strength and Shield.

When I tread the verge of Jordan,
Bid my anxious fears subside;
Death of death and hell's Destruction,
Land me safe on Canaan's side;
Songs of praises, songs of praises
I will ever give to Thee,
I will ever give to Thee.

William Williams[6]

Choking

Anxiety robs us of the privilege of being grateful neighbors. *Anxiety* means to strangle or choke. When our throat is cut off, we cannot eat and will become malnourished. Worry chokes out our joy and thanksgiving. The Lord went straight to the heart after teaching the disciples how to pray. He addressed our issues of chronic anxiety about His future provision in the Sermon on the Mount. What we identify as our most pressing needs—drink, food, or clothing—can consume all our thinking. He encourages us to look at His creation: the birds, lilies, and grass, and at His glorious display of provision. The reality is we should care more about how we live than how we eat; the spiritual should go before the physical, the eternal before the temporal. Worrying about temporal needs is not the orientation of a dependent daughter. We are children of the King. He is omniscient and has intimate knowledge. Our perfect Parent knows what we need better than we do ourselves. We must ask Him to search us before we seek Him (Ps. 139:23). We get distracted, so Jesus encourages us to seek His kingdom. This is a single-minded focus. Seeking first His kingdom orientates us around the priority on God's glory. And when we are captivated by Him, all these needful things will be added unto us. The overflow is God's provision for our good. Anxiety is always focused on tomorrow or the future, so Jesus tells us to focus on today and pray for daily bread. "But seek first the kingdom of God and His righteousness, and all these things will be added to you. Therefore, do not be anxious about tomorrow, for tomorrow will be anxious for itself. Sufficient for the day is its own trouble" (Matt. 6:33-34).

> We shy away from prayers that invite God to rule our lives. They make us vulnerable.
>
> Paul Miller[7]

Lots to Learn

I would like to tell you after all these years, I am further along at learning to be dependent, content, free from anxiety, and full of generosity. But God is not finished with this neighbor. I still have much to learn. My prayer life often shrinks to the level of this discipleship gap in my life. Why don't I pray, "Give us this day our daily bread"? Here are just a few things the Spirit has taught me over the years.

- I don't pray, because deep down I don't really believe I am needy. I am comfortable in my self-sufficient world that I seek to control.
- I would rather spin in anxiety, grasping for next month's bread than sit in prayer.
- I am either too prideful or full of shame to ask my brothers and sisters to pray this along with me.
- I take my daily nourishment for granted. I complain about the scarcity of my "greeds" instead of sharing generously out of His daily meeting my needs.
- I become deluded and believe I can actually supply all my needs according to my own schemes and resources—that I am the source and sustainer of my life rather than my Father.

My prayerlessness reveals at my core I do not love God with all my heart, soul, mind, and strength, and I have failed to love my neighbor. But the good news is we serve a Father who loves to answer His kids' prayers. As His kingdom comes in my heart and His will is done, my heart is transformed, enabling me to come more humbly and consistently to pray, "Give us this day's bread."

Weekly Prayer List

Write the Lord's Prayer over your life this week. Spend time writing out your prayer requests in these four areas. Come back to this list daily to continue to ask, seek, or knock. Put a star next to answered prayers. And then on day seven, reflect and praise God for what He has done and allow the remaining items to shape your prayers for next week.

Our Father in heaven, hallowed be Your name. Your kingdom come, Your will be done, on earth as it is in heaven. Give us this day our daily bread, and forgive us our debts, as we also have forgiven our debtors. And lead us not into temptation, but deliver us from evil (Matt. 6:9-13).

Personal Prayer

Family Prayer

Church Prayer

Prayer for my neighbors (work or community)

Day One: Gratitude

INHALE GOD'S WORD

His kingdom comes, and His will is done when we give thanks. "Give thanks in all circumstances; for this is the will of God in Christ Jesus for you" (1 Thess. 5:18).

Read the following verses from Psalms and fill this treasure chest with His provisions that should cause our hearts and mouths to overflow with thanks.

Read:

- Psalm 7:17
- Psalm 9:1
- Psalm 28:7
- Psalm 75:1
- Psalm 95:1-2
- Psalm 100
- Psalm 106:1
- Psalm 107:1
- Psalm 118

EXHALE IN PRAYER ~ ADORATION

Dear Generous Father, my heart is full of thanksgiving for the following things. . .

GO BACK TO YOUR WEEKLY PRAYER LIST AND SPEND TIME IN PRAYER.

Day Two: Give

INHALE GOD'S WORD

Go back and read the entire story in Exodus 16 of how God provided for His hungry children in the wilderness. Spend time reflecting on the following questions:

In what ways have you believed in the ideology of scarcity, grumbling, and complaining about the "not-enoughness" in your life?

How has God provided daily bread or manna in your life? List everything needful for life He has provided this week.

Have you been tempted to hoard your "daily bread" for tomorrow's care? List ways that this human scheming leads to rottenness.

What are one or two ways you can intentionally remember His provision in your life (like Moses placing the omer of manna in the ark of the covenant)?

EXHALE IN PRAYER ~ ADORATION

Dear God, who provided in the wilderness, thank You for providing for me in all these ways . . .

GO BACK TO YOUR WEEKLY PRAYER LIST AND SPEND TIME IN PRAYER.

Day Three: Us

INHALE GOD'S WORD

Read and reflect on Question #104 from the *Westminster Shorter Catechism.*[8]

Q. 104: What do we pray for in the fourth petition?

A: In the fourth petition, which is, *Give us this day our daily bread*, we pray that of God's free gift we may receive a competent portion of the good things of this life, and enjoy His blessing with them.

Read these scripture proofs that underscore God's provision for you.

Proverbs 30:8-9

Matthew 6:31-34

Philippians 4:11-14, 19-20

1 Timothy 6:6-8

EXHALE IN PRAYER ~ CONFESSION

Dear Generous Father, I confess that I have not been content with all You have provided in these areas . . .

GO BACK TO YOUR WEEKLY PRAYER LIST AND SPEND TIME IN PRAYER.

Day Four: Prayer Book – The Psalms

INHALE GOD'S WORD

Read Psalm 34. Taste and see that the Lord is good! Write nourishing truths from this passage about God's character on each slice of bread. Now pray about how you can share this nourishment with others this week.

EXHALE IN PRAYER ~ THANKSGIVING

Dear Gracious Provider, I thank You for all the ways you have blessed and provided for me this week, including . . .

GO BACK TO YOUR WEEKLY PRAYER LIST AND SPEND TIME IN PRAYER.

Day Five: This Day

INHALE GOD'S WORD

Read Psalm 127:1-2, Matthew 6:25-34, Philippians 4:6-7, and 1 Peter 5:5-8.
Spend an extended time considering what cares you are carrying that God never intended for you to carry. How can you come humbly and actively cast them onto the Father, trusting He will supply all your needs according to His riches in glory?

CASTING PARTY

Cares and burdens I am not meant to carry	What it will look like to cast these onto Christ and trust Him to provide this week

EXHALE IN PRAYER ~ CONFESSION

Dear Compassionate Father, I repent of carrying these burdens You never intended me to carry. Would You enable me to trust You to provide in the following. . .

GO BACK TO YOUR WEEKLY PRAYER LIST AND SPEND TIME IN PRAYER.

Day Six: Contentment

INHALE GOD'S WORD

Read 2 Corinthians 12:9-10, Philippians 4:11-13, 1 Timothy 6:6, and Hebrews 13:5.
Spend time journaling below about your own contentment classroom over the last year.

Name periods of plenty and want over the past year.

Name two or three ways you have learned the secret like Paul.

Name two or three ways His strength has been perfected in your weakness.

Name two or three ways godliness paired with contentment has been great gain in your life over the past year.

EXHALE IN PRAYER ~ THANKSGIVING

Dear Sovereign Lord, thank You for Your patience in teaching me contentment in the following ways . . . .

GO BACK TO YOUR WEEKLY PRAYER LIST AND SPEND TIME IN PRAYER.

Day Seven: Writing His Prayer over Your Life

INHALE GOD'S WORD

Read back through our passage for this week, Matthew 6:11.

What are three takeaways you learned this week through your personal study, prayer journaling, or your small group discussion?

1.

2.

3.

EXHALE IN PRAYER ~ SUPPLICATION

Dear Generous Father, would You write Your prayer over my life, family, church, and neighbors. . .

RETURN TO YOUR WEEKLY PRAYER LIST

- Place a star next to answered prayers.
- Spend time giving praise to God.
- Reflect upon His persevering grace for what remains on your prayer list.
- Ask God to apply what you have learned this week as you seek His face to write your prayer list for next week.

1 Brené Brown, *Daring Greatly* (New York, NY: Penguin Publishing, 2015), 25.

2 Richard Coekin, *Our Father: Enjoying God in Prayer* (Downers Grove, IL: Intervarsity Press, 2009), 110.

3 Spiros Zodhiates, *The Lord's Prayer* (Chattanooga, TN: AMG Publishers, 1998), 178-179.

4 J.I. Packer, *Praying the Lord's Prayer* (Wheaton, IL: Crossway, 2007), 74.

5 John Calvin, *Commentary on a Harmony of Evangelists: Matthew, Mark, and Luke*, trans. William Pringle, 3 vols (1979 reprint, Grand Rapids: Baker Book House), 1:314.

6 William Williams, "Guide Me, O Thou Great Jehovah!" in *Trinity Hymnal* (Suwanee, GA: Great Commission Publications, 2021), 598.

7 Paul Miller, *A Praying Life* (Colorado Springs, CO: NavPress, 2009), 145.

8 *The Westminster Shorter Catechism* (Lawrenceville GA: Committee on Discipleship Ministries, 1990), 33.

Week Six:
Protection

Learning to pray as a Forgiven Follower

Matthew 6:12-13

Teaching
WEEKLY FOCUS & IDENTITY THEMES

Matthew 6:12-13

. . . and forgive us our debts, as we also have forgiven our debtors.
And lead us not into temptation, but deliver us from evil.

Bondage

Unforgiveness is a prison cell. Before Christ, I was trapped by habitual sins and imprisoned by shame over my past. I sat in a dark, stinking prison cell, a hostage of Satan, awaiting a death sentence. I gazed through the bars, wondering what life was like outside. I thought if I worked hard enough to get God to love me more, then I could escape. But I felt trapped and deep in debt. I was in bondage, and it seemed impossible to leave. Because the cell was so dark, I couldn't see or smell how dirty, filthy, and stinky I had become.

But there is good news! The gospel tells me on the cross, Christ paid the ransom to open the door to my cell. He paid my debt and redeemed me with His precious blood. His forgiveness grants me freedom! I blink and squint as He brings me out into the light. I can clearly see how filthy I have become, but I also see how beautiful life lived in the Light can be. He cleanses me and puts on me robes of pure white righteousness. Still, there are days when I struggle with temptations and sin. I am also tempted to crawl back into the dark, dirty cell. When I do, although familiar, it ultimately becomes unbearable, and it makes me miserable.

The forgiveness of Christ has not only paid to set me free, but it keeps me permanently free. He uses His Word and the prayers of His people to guide me and lead me in the everlasting way back into the light. I pray for His kingdom to come and His will to be done in the now-and-not-yet. These prayers transform me in the midst of the struggle. One day He will come again and close the door behind me, and I will never return to the filthy cell again. I will be free forever!

This week we wrap up our study on the Lord's Prayer. Our lesson begins with the word "and." This little conjunction connects all these final petitions that focus on man's needs together. They are all essential for life and godliness. We need them daily—food for the body, forgiveness for our souls, and deliverance from evil.

An equally important insight is a reminder that the Lord's Prayer is given to us in plural form. We ask God to give us what we need. Prayer is not strictly a private thing. As much as we can, we should pray with others both formally in gathered worship and informally. Why? If the substance of prayer is to continue a conversation with God, and if the purpose of it is to know God better, then this can happen best in community.

Tim Keller[1]

Spiritual Bankruptcy

As in my opening illustration, there can often be a gap between our perceived condition and our actual condition. Without Christ, our condition is pretty bleak. We are in bondage as debtors. Debtors are people who are beholden to others. They are bound to them by some kind of obligation. Perhaps you have purchased something on credit; you get the gist of being in debt. Sometimes, people seek a financial counselor to calculate the extent of their total indebtedness. You have to know how much you owe in order to know how much you have to pay. But here is the problem: without Christ, we are drowning in debt. We have the debt of original sin. "For as by the one man's disobedience the many were made sinners, so by the one man's obedience the many will be made righteous" (Rom. 5:19).

Sin makes us all debtors to God. Since we cannot pay by our works, we are imprisoned, and there is no release date without divine intervention. Praying "and forgive us our debts," puts the finger on our desire to be justified through our self-righteousness. Again, we see the glory-gap as we pray and marvel at the greatness and goodness of our loving Father. God is holy, and we are not. He cannot just overlook sin. Debts have to be paid. We are spiritually bankrupt and squarely in arrears to God. The cost of sin is so high, we can't afford to pay it. "Truly no man can ransom another, or give to God the price of his life, for the ransom of their life is costly and can never suffice" (Ps. 49:7-8). But the good news is Christ paid the penalty for sin in full. His last words were, "It is finished" (John 19:30).

In this prayer everything hinges on another little conjunction, "as." This little word sets up the grand compare-and-contrast: "as we also have forgiven our debtors." Forgiveness is a pattern we set that is contingent on the degree we are willing to forgive. Christ is teaching us that we are asking God to forgive us by the same pattern we forgive others. This is another dangerous petition to pray. Another way of thinking about this is we are saying, "God deal with me the way I deal with others." If we want to enjoy the benefits of God's forgiveness towards us, we must be willing to forgive others, even those who repeatedly sin against us.

Jesus told a parable about a Pharisee and a tax collector which exposes the true condition of their hearts by the nature of their prayers.

> *"Two men went up into the temple to pray, one a Pharisee and the other a tax collector. The Pharisee, standing by himself, prayed thus: 'God, I thank you that I am not like other men, extortioners, unjust, adulterers, or even like this tax collector. I fast twice a week; I give tithes of all that I get.' But the tax collector, standing far off, would not even lift up his eyes to heaven, but beat his breast, saying, 'God, be merciful to me, a sinner!' I tell you; this man went down to his house justified, rather than the other. For everyone who exalts himself will be humbled, but the one who humbles himself will be exalted"* (Luke 18:10-14).

We learned in Week One our position in Christ determines our posture in prayer. The Pharisee had a prideful posture. He was praying to be seen and to promote his reputation. He made much of himself with no mention of the Father. The tax collector's posture was humble and contrite. He could not even lift his eyes to heaven. His first word was "God," rather than about himself or his needs. We may be tempted to minimize or conceal our sin. Confession is at the core of prayer.

The gospel illuminates our hearts to see our true condition. We can look into the mirror of His Word and not run back into bondage but instead run into the loving arms of the Father. The tax collector's prayer is that of a forgiven follower, "God, be merciful to me, a sinner!" "Forgive us our debts!" God answers this prayer by telling us to "humble yourselves before the Lord, and He will exalt you" (James 4:10). The hymn writer Elvina Hall wrote, "Jesus paid it all. All to Him I owe." Because of our debt we need a surety, like a co-signer of the loan. Jesus is our surety, and salvation is not cheap. Because of our disobedience and inability to keep the law, we carry a spiritual IOU. Forgiveness is canceling of the IOU. "Without the shedding of blood there is no forgiveness of sins" (Heb. 9:22).

To forgive is to set a prisoner free and discover that the prisoner was you.

Lewis Smedes[2]

Forgiveness

Unforgiveness is not just a prison cell for you in your sin, but you are also held in bondage when you refuse to forgive another. The ability to forgive is one of the surest signs we have been forgiven. Maybe you too have wondered, like Peter, how many times can I be expected to forgive someone who habitually sins against me? Jesus answered Peter's question with a parable about the cost of unforgiveness.

> *Then Peter came up and said to Him, "Lord, how often will my brother sin against me, and I forgive him? As many as seven times?" Jesus said to him, "I do not say to you seven times, but seventy-seven times.*
>
> *"Therefore, the kingdom of heaven may be compared to a king who wished to settle accounts with his servants. When he began to settle, one was brought to him who owed him ten thousand talents. And since he could not pay, his master ordered him to be sold, with his wife and children and all that he had, and payment to be made. So, the servant fell on his knees, imploring him, 'Have patience with me, and I will pay you everything.' And out of pity for him, the master of that servant released him and forgave him the debt. But when that same servant went out, he found one of his fellow servants who owed him a hundred denarii, and seizing him, he began to choke him, saying, 'Pay what you owe.' So, his fellow servant fell down and pleaded with him, 'Have patience with me, and I will pay you.' He refused and went and put him in prison until he should pay the debt. When his fellow servants saw what had taken place, they were greatly distressed, and they went and reported to their master all that had taken place. Then his master summoned him and said to him, 'You wicked servant! I forgave you all that debt because you pleaded with me. And should not you have had mercy on your fellow servant, as I had mercy on you?' And in anger his master delivered him to the jailers, until he should pay all his debt. So also, my heavenly Father will do to every one of you, if you do not forgive your brother from your heart"* (Matt. 18:21-35).

We do not receive forgiveness because we forgive others, but because we cast ourselves on the mercy of God. Yet we cannot receive forgiveness without forgiving others. The man who mouths the words, "forgive us our debts" but will not forgive others their debt has not begun to understand the weight of his own sin.

Sinclair Ferguson[3]

The king's forgiveness has the priority. He extends forgiveness first. There is nothing the servant (or we) can do to deserve it. The king's heart is full of mercy. The servant feels he is unable to forgive because he has never entered into the mercy of the Father. He begged for his debt to be canceled without understanding how much he owed. He had failed to calculate how much forgiveness costs. We cannot work for forgiveness; we must ask for forgiveness. Since the servant was unwilling to forgive, he was unable to be forgiven. We serve a King who lives in heaven. We hallow His name as we reflect His magnanimous heart. His kingdom comes, and His will is done when we extend mercy and forgiveness.

Forgiveness means to let go, release from debt without a sense of guilt, obligation, or punishment. Forgiveness, at its center is a matter of fellowship. "Forgive us" points to the reality that if I am not in fellowship with God and others, I cannot effectively pray. We must consider the cost of forgiveness. It will cost my laying down my rights, having the last word, the protecting of my reputation, and keeping an account of wrongs. But what will it cost me to not forgive? A heart that refuses to forgive fellow believers will be robbed of its joy, peace, fellowship, and usefulness in the Church. It has been said unforgiveness is like a poison we drink. It hardens the heart and can lead to anger and bitterness, especially if we rehearse the offense over and over. It can also impact us emotionally and physically, leading to stress, anxiety, depression, insecurity, and fear. Forgiveness is the key that is placed in the lock of the prison. We unshackle ourselves from the offense and the debtor when we choose to forgive others.

The deliverance we need is not only or mainly from adverse circumstances, but from the spiritual evil within us that makes both adverse and favorable circumstances its springboard for attack. Sin in our hearts, spawning all kinds of inclinations to do something other than God's will and to love something or someone more than God Himself, is the source of our danger.

J.I. Packer[4]

Battlefield

The Lord's Prayer instructs us to pray about our food, forgiveness, and fragility. There can also be a gap between our perceived safety and the hazards of sin. We intercede for our safety as well as that of our brothers and sisters when we pray, "And lead us not into temptation, but deliver us from evil." We live on a battlefield, so we must kneel in prayer with a wartime mentality.

Christ is our Leader, and we look to Him for our footing in this fallen world. This petition has two parts. We ask the Lord to keep us from temptations that cause us to stray off the path of obedience and to deliver us from evil when it threatens to undo us. Temptations and evil attack us on three fronts. The nature of our enemy is the world, the flesh, and the devil. The culture of this world seeks to oppose the truth. Secularism, individualism, and materialism are the polluted air we breathe. This world is foreign to us because it is not our Home. "If you were of the world, the world would love you as its own; but because you are not of the world, but I chose you out of the world, therefore the world hates you" (John 15:19). Evil is closer than we can imagine. The New Testament draws the battlefield of the now-and-not-yet struggle. There is an ongoing war between the flesh and the Spirit. Our fallen nature is a tenacious foe. Prayer leads us to repentance and faith to put to death the sin that so easily entangles us. "For the desires of the flesh are against the Spirit, and the desires of the Spirit are against the flesh, for these are opposed to each other, to keep you from doing the things you want to do" (Gal. 5:17). And the sneakiest enemy of all is the devil. He will not have the victory, but he lives to stir up trouble in us and within the Church. We must be on the alert, ready to resist Him by the Spirit. "Be sober-minded; be watchful. Your adversary the devil prowls around like a roaring lion, seeking someone to devour" (1 Peter 5:8). God answers this prayer by giving us a way to escape. "No temptation has overtaken you that is not common to man. God is faithful, and He will not let you be tempted beyond your ability, but with the temptation He will also provide the way of escape, that you may be able to endure it" (1 Cor. 10:13). In His high priestly prayer, Christ prayed for our protection from the evil one. "I do not ask that You take them out of the world, but that You keep them from the evil one" (John 17:15).

A Mighty Fortress

A mighty fortress is our God, a bulwark never failing;
Our Helper He, amid the flood of mortal ills prevailing.
For still our ancient foe doth seek to work us woe;
His craft and power are great; and armed with cruel hate,
On earth is not his equal.

Did we in our own strength confide, our striving would be losing;
Were not the right Man on our side, the Man of God's own choosing.
Dost ask who that may be? Christ Jesus, it is He,
The Lord Sabaoth His name, from age to age the same,
And He must win the battle.

And though this world, with devils filled, should threaten to undo us,
We will not fear, for God hath willed His truth to triumph through us.
The prince of darkness grim, we tremble not for him;
His rage we can endure, for lo! his doom is sure;
One little word shall fell him.

That Word above all earthly powers, no thanks to them, abideth;
The Spirit and the gifts are ours through Him who with us sideth.
Let goods and kindred go, this mortal life also;
The body they may kill; God's truth abideth still;
His kingdom is forever.

Martin Luther[5]

Praying the Lord's Prayer is for weak, vulnerable, forgiven followers. Our position in Christ will determine our posture in prayer and our stance on the battlefield. The battle is won or lost in our minds and hearts. "We destroy arguments and every lofty opinion raised against the knowledge of God, and take every thought captive to obey Christ" (2 Cor. 10:5). We fight evil and temptation on our knees. Spiritual warfare happens as we battle between the old man (walking in the flesh) and the new man (walking in the Spirit). We must become keenly aware of our potential vulnerabilities which leave us open to being wounded. We are susceptible to the enemy when we rest in self-sufficiency. We risk attack when we are passive in our spiritual walk instead of active. When we forget to preach the truth of the gospel to ourselves, we are exposed to the father of lies.

Our call to arms is written here. "Finally, be strong in the Lord and in the strength of His might. Put on the whole armor of God, that you may be able to stand against the schemes of the devil. For we do not wrestle against flesh and blood, but against the rulers, against the authorities, against the cosmic powers over this present darkness, against the spiritual forces of evil in the heavenly places. Therefore take up the whole armor of God, that you may be able to withstand in the evil day, and having done all, to stand firm. Stand therefore, having fastened on the belt of truth, and having put on the breastplate of righteousness, and, as shoes for your feet, having put on the readiness given by the gospel of peace. In all circumstances take up the shield of faith, with which you can extinguish all the flaming darts of the evil one; and take the helmet of salvation, and the sword of the Spirit, which is the word of God" (Eph. 6:10-17).

We are called to be strong in the Lord, in His strength not our own. We are not left defenseless, but we are given the armor of the Lord. It covers us from head to toe and protects us from the fiery darts of the evil one. And when temptations and evils come—and they will—we are called to stand firm. We are ready to be on the defense because the gospel of peace gives us support and stability. Our walk is not reactive, but proactive. Reading and memorizing God's Word is an offensive weapon that helps gain the victory over sin in our lives. It doesn't just protect; it maims. The Word isn't passive; it's living and active (Heb. 4:12). It is intended for combat—a weapon for frontline spiritual warfare.

And this fight brings us back to prayer: "praying at all times in the Spirit, with all prayer and supplication. To that end, keep alert with all perseverance, making supplication for all the saints" (Eph. 6:18). This prayer is to be spiritual prayer: "In the Spirit." It is to be watchful prayer: "Keep alert." And it is to be intercessory prayer: "Making supplication for all the saints." We are praying the Lord will make all of us faithful followers and lead us. We pray He will guard our hearts and minds from tempting thoughts and deeds and He will "lead us not into temptation," and He will "deliver us from evil" and lead us in the everlasting way. "Search me, O God, and know my heart! Try me and know my thoughts! And see if there be any grievous way in me, and lead me in the way everlasting" (Ps. 139:23-24)!

> The older I get, the more I want to sing my faith and get others singing it with me. Theology is for doxology: the first thing to do with it is to turn it into praise and thus honor the God who is its subject.
>
> J.I. Packer[6]

Doxology

When we say the Lord's Prayer in church, we often end with this doxology: "For Yours is the kingdom, and the power, and the glory, forever. A-men." This ending is not included in Matthew's Gospel, but most likely was added as a hymnic addition to facilitate a worshipful reading of the passage in the early Church. So, as we come to the end of our study, I pray your heart will sing, and you will worship Him for all He has taught you. *Yours, O Lord, is the kingdom!* "Your kingdom is an everlasting kingdom, and Your dominion endures throughout all generations. The Lord is faithful in all His words and kind in all His works" (Ps. 145:13). *Yours, O Lord, is the power!* "Great is our Lord, and abundant in power; His understanding is beyond measure" (Ps. 147:5) *Yours, O Lord, is the glory!* "Now to Him who is able to do far more abundantly than all that we ask or think, according to the power at work within us" (Eph. 3:20). *Forever. A-men!* I agree with this prayer, may it be so in my life.

Praying the Lord's Prayer is a dangerous prayer. It always brings changes. It transforms our words, deeds, and actions. It unites and grows our relationships with our brothers and sisters in Christ. It holds within it the power to revolutionize our homes and workplaces. As we faithfully pray, the world around us begins to morph as His kingdom comes and His will is done. It has also been transformative to reflect on how our positions in Christ determine our posture in prayer. I leave you with my prayers for you. I pray you will take time to reflect on how understanding your adoption as a dependent daughter propels you to run needy, messy, and often to your Father. May you be encouraged that you are not alone but are a part of God's big family as an interdependent sister who can cry out, "Our Father" because we are privileged to live proximate to Him. I intercede for you to press on hallowing His name in your life as a holy pilgrim whose trajectory is Home. I ask boldly that He would enable you to be a loyal steward with all He has entrusted you with as you pray corporately for His kingdom to come and His will to be done on earth as it is in heaven. I pray for your heart to be filled to overflowing with thanksgiving as you seek to freely share His daily provision of bread with others as a grateful neighbor. And finally, I pray the Spirit will enable you to live in freedom while you stay alert under His protective love as He leads you not into temptation but delivers you from evil as a forgiven follower of Christ. I exhort you to daily write the Lord's Prayer over your lives, homes, work, church, and community. May the Lord's Prayer become the life-giving, essential oxygen of your life. Breathe!

Weekly Prayer List

Write the Lord's Prayer over your life this week. Spend time writing out your prayer requests in these four areas. Come back to this list daily to continue to ask, seek, or knock. Put a star next to answered prayers. And then on day seven, reflect and praise God for what He has done and allow the remaining items to shape your prayers for next week.

Our Father in heaven, hallowed be Your name. Your kingdom come, Your will be done, on earth as it is in heaven. Give us this day our daily bread, and forgive us our debts, as we also have forgiven our debtors. And lead us not into temptation, but deliver us from evil (Matt. 6:9-13).

Personal Prayer

Family Prayer

Church Prayer

Prayer for my neighbors (work or community)

Day One: Forgiveness

INHALE GOD'S WORD

Read Psalm 130, Ephesians 4:32, Colossians 2:13-14, and 1 John 4:7-11.
Journal the blessings of forgiveness.
Meditate on what forgiveness is and what forgiveness is not. Write your own comparisons.

FORGIVENESS IS.....	FORGIVENESS IS NOT....
A choice we make	A feeling we have
Supernatural act	Our natural default
Unconditional	Conditional
Acknowledging the offense but forgiving it	Excusing unjust behavior
Sincere and from the heart	Trite and just sweeping it under the rug
Something that flows out from the mercy we received	Something we achieve by being nice, and it flows from our good works

EXHALE IN PRAYER ~ ADORATION

Dear Forgiving Father, I praise You for Your tender mercies towards me in the following things. . .

GO BACK TO YOUR WEEKLY PRAYER LIST AND SPEND TIME IN PRAYER.

Day Two: Unforgiveness

INHALE GOD'S WORD

Read the following consequences of unforgiveness.

- Our prayers will not be answered: Psalm 66:18-19
- The Holy Spirit is grieved: Ephesians 4:30
- The Devil gains a foothold in our life: Ephesians 4:27
- You may grow bitter: Ephesians 4:31
- You can get entangled by sin, hindering you from running the race of faith: Hebrews 12:1

Spend time in prayer asking yourself:
Is there anyone I need to ask for their forgiveness?

Am I holding a grudge against anyone?

Am I actively rehearsing wrongs done against me?

Do I harbor any bitterness against anyone?

How can I seek to remember the forgiveness that Christ extended to me and extend it to others? To whom?

EXHALE IN PRAYER ~ ADORATION

Dear, God, I thank You for purchasing my forgiveness on the cross. It is a blessing to me in these ways . . .

GO BACK TO YOUR WEEKLY PRAYER LIST AND SPEND TIME IN PRAYER.

Day Three: Forgive, Lead, & Deliver

INHALE GOD'S WORD

Read and reflect on the scripture proofs from the *Heidelberg Catechism* Questions #126 and 127. [7]

Q. 126: What does the fifth petition mean?

A: "Forgive us our debts, as we also have forgiven our debtors" means: Because of Christ's blood, do not hold against us, poor sinners that we are, any of the sins we do or the evil that constantly clings to us (Ps. 51:1-7; 143:2; Rom.8:1; 1 John 2:1-2). Forgive us just as we are fully determined, as evidence of Your grace in us, to forgive our neighbors (Matt. 6:14-15; 18:21-35).

Q. 127: What does the sixth petition mean?

A: "And do not bring us to the time of trial, but rescue us from the evil one" means: By ourselves we are too weak to hold our own even for a moment (Ps. 103:14-16; John 15:1-5). And our sworn enemies—the devil (Eph. 6:10-13; 1 Peter 5:8), the world (John 15:18-21), and our own flesh (Rom. 7:23; Gal. 5:17)—never stop attacking us. And so, Lord, uphold us and make us strong with the strength of Your Holy Spirit, so that we may not go down to defeat in this spiritual struggle (Matt. 10:19-20; Mark 13:33; Rom. 5:3-5), but may firmly resist our enemies until we finally win the complete victory (1 Cor. 10:13; 1 Thess. 3:13; 5:23).

EXHALE IN PRAYER ~ CONFESSION

Dear Kind and Loving Father, I confess that I have not forgiven others the way You have forgiven me in the following relationships. . .

GO BACK TO YOUR WEEKLY PRAYER LIST AND SPEND TIME IN PRAYER.

Day Four: Prayer Book – The Psalms

INHALE GOD'S WORD

Read Psalm 139 and write the action words that describe God's protection and care of you as He leads you not into temptation, delivers you from evil, and leads you in His everlasting path.

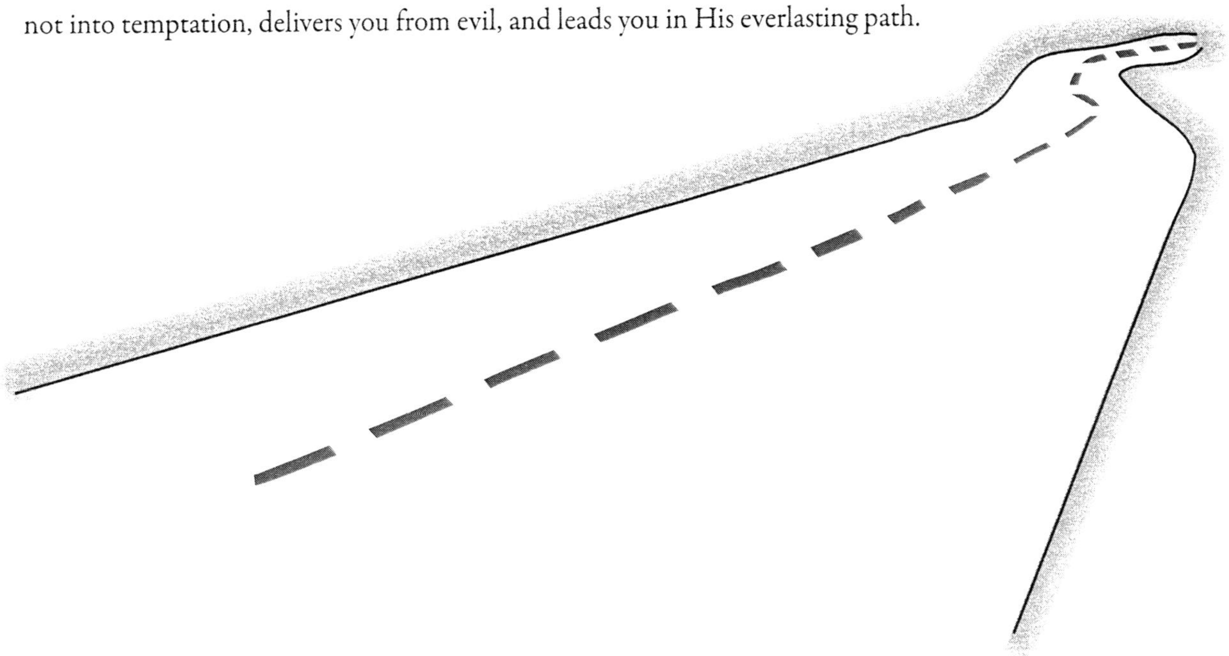

EXHALE IN PRAYER ~ THANKSGIVING

Dear Faithful Holy Spirit, I thank You for these specific ways you have led me this week to follow You. . .

GO BACK TO YOUR WEEKLY PRAYER LIST AND SPEND TIME IN PRAYER.

Day Five: Temptation

INHALE GOD'S WORD

Read Matthew 4:1-11 about the temptation of Christ by Satan. Reflect on the following questions.

In what ways have you hungered for power to meet your own needs?

In what ways have you arrogantly put God to the test?

What are two or three scriptures you can apply this week to resist temptation?

EXHALE IN PRAYER ~ CONFESSION

Dear Compassionate Father, I repent of not standing firm on Your Word to resist the following evil desires . . .

GO BACK TO YOUR WEEKLY PRAYER LIST AND SPEND TIME IN PRAYER.

Day Six: Doxology

INHALE GOD'S WORD

Read the following passages, reflect on the questions, and let your heart sing with praises to the King of kings.

Yours, O Lord, is the kingdom: Psalm 145:13
How have you sought to set up your own kingdom?

Yours, O Lord, is the power: Psalm 147:5
How is His power perfected in your powerlessness?

Yours, O Lord, is the glory: Psalm 3:3
In what ways have you sought self-glory over God's glory?

EXHALE IN PRAYER ~ THANKSGIVING

Dear King of kings, I thank You for Your kingdom, power and glory. Would You show them to me this week in the following ways . . .

GO BACK TO YOUR WEEKLY PRAYER LIST AND SPEND TIME IN PRAYER.

Day Seven: Writing His Prayer over Your Life

INHALE GOD'S WORD

Read back through our passage for this study, Matthew 6:5-13.

What are your big three takeaways from the entire study?

1.

2.

3.

EXHALE IN PRAYER ~ SUPPLICATION

Dear Generous Father, would You write Your prayer over my life, family, church, and neighbors. . .

RETURN TO YOUR WEEKLY PRAYER LIST

- Place a star next to answered prayers.
- Spend time giving praise to God.
- Reflect upon His persevering grace for what remains on your prayer list.
- Ask God to apply what you have learned this week as you seek His face to write your prayer lists in the weeks to come.

1 Tim Keller, *Prayer: Experiencing Awe and Intimacy with God* (New York, NY: Penguin Books, 2014), 188-199.

2 "Lewis B. Smedes Quotes," BrainyQuote.com, BrainyMedia Inc, accessed 19 February 2022, https://www.brainyquote.com/quotes/lewis_b_smedes_135524.

3 Sinclair Ferguson, *The Sermon on the Mount* (Edinburgh: Banner of Truth, 1987), 130.

4 J.I. Packer, *Praying the Lord's Prayer* (Wheaton, IL: Crossway, 2007), 94.

5 Martin Luther, "A Mighty Fortress Is Our God" in *Trinity Hymnal* (Suwanee, GA: Great Commission Publications, 2021), 92.

6 J.I. Packer, *God Has Spoken: Revelation and the Bible* (Ada, MI: Baker Books, 2012), 7.

7 G.I. Williamson, *The Heidelberg Catechism: A Study Guide* (Phillipsburg, NJ: P&R Publishing, 1993), 227, 230.

The content for the six-week, online curriculum, *Building on the Lord's Prayer*, has been modified from Heather Molendyk's *Building Little Pillars*, which introduces children to the spiritual truths found in the Apostles' Creed, the Ten Commandments, and the Lord's Prayer. Through the teaching of sound Reformed doctrines, *Building Little Pillars* lays a firm foundation for covenant children as they begin their journey of faith.

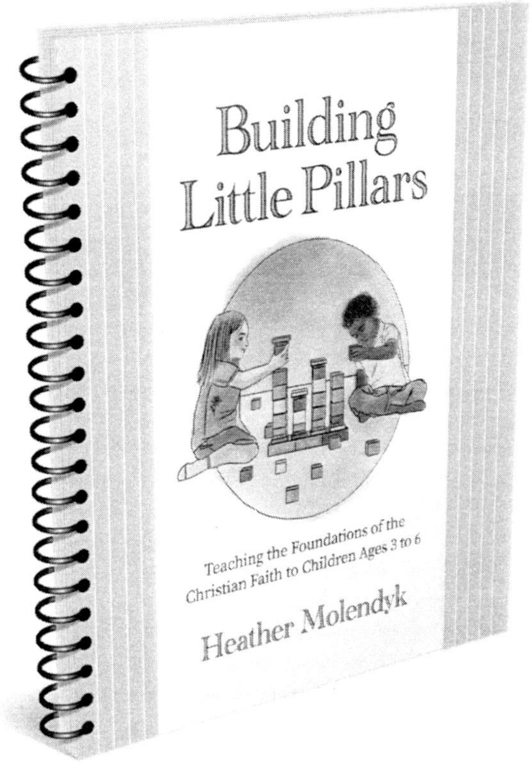

Building Little Pillars is available in hard copy or as a pdf download from the PCA Bookstore, www.pcabookstore.com.

cdm™
Presbyterian Church in America
DISCIPLESHIP MINISTRIES
1700 North Brown Road | Suite 102 | Lawrenceville, Georgia 30043
www.pcabookstore.com | 1.800.283.1357